PRAISE FOR DRE

"If you are intrigued by dream work of any kind, this book will take you through the process step by step. It is packed with practical information, insight, and guidance for not just the usual dream work but also other areas such as using dreams for a purpose. Practical and enlightening."

—**RACHEL PATTERSON**, bestselling author of more than twenty-five books on Witchcraft and Paganism

"A mesmerizing journey through the moonlit corridors of your subconscious, unlocking the hidden treasures of your dreams to fill your nights with magick. This book enchants with its methods for dream recall, intuitive and prophetic dreaming, and lucid exploration. Corak's guidance will empower you to transform nightmares into powerful allies. As you summon dream allies, craft protective charms, and embark on guided journeys to astral realms, you'll find a place where creativity and insight glow like starlight, shadows reveal their wisdom, and the spirit world whispers its secrets."

—**MAT AURYN**, author of *Psychic Witch*, *Mastering Magick*, and *The Psychic Art of Tarot*

"A valuable journey through the body, mind, and spirit into the landscapes of dreaming. From cultural context to specific practices to enhance your recall and expand your interpretation abilities, this book is perfect for those who are just starting to track their dreamtime, as well as for those who want to deepen these practices. Corak offers a comprehensive guide for the liminal spaces and ensures a reader does not go to these places alone."

—**IRISANYA MOON**, author of *Artemis: Goddess of the Wild Hunt*

"An engaging exploration into the esoteric world of dreaming. Both concise and richly informative, *Dream Magick* is of benefit to Pagans and occultists whose waking lives are influenced by the dreamworld. Packed with fascinating history and practical workings, this book helps readers engage with the subtle workings of the psyche and spirit."
—RAVEN DIGITALIS, author of *The Empath's Oracle*

"A brilliant blend of the science, history, and magic that lies within dreams. Corak skillfully talks the reader through the entire process of developing the craft of using dreams in a magical practice, from the setup to the follow-through. There is so much information packed into this work, and useful exercises and ideas for you to explore…She shares her own personal experiences with different aspects of dreaming, which not only make the practices relatable, but also give this work a real personable approach."
—JOANNA VAN DER HOEVEN, author of *The Path of the Hedge Witch* and *The Book of Hedge Druidry*

DREAM

MAGICK

ABOUT THE AUTHOR

Robin Corak has been fascinated with dreams for most of her life and is a member of the International Association for the Study of Dreams. A practicing Pagan for more than twenty-five years, Robin is a skilled tarot reader and Reiki practitioner as well as a certified end of life doula. She has presented at multiple national and international conferences, writes a blog for Patheos Agora and has previously authored two books entitled *Persephone: Practicing the Art of Personal Power* (Moon Books, 2020) and *Demeter* (Moon Books, 2022). Robin is a longtime member of the Sisterhood of Avalon and recently retired as the CEO of a large social services nonprofit organization in Washington state. Find out more about Robin via her website, www.phoenixawenrising.com or via social media on Facebook (https://www.facebook.com/robin.corak) and Instagram (https://www.instagram.com/robincorak/).

DREAM

MAGICK

Change Your Reality through the Liminal World of Sleep

ROBIN CORAK

LLEWELLYN
WOODBURY, MINNESOTA

FIRST EDITION
First Printing, 2024

Book design by R. Brasington
Cover design by Kevin R. Brown
Editing by Laura Kurtz
Interior illustrations by Llewellyn Art Department on pages: 126, 138, 142

Llewellyn Publications is a registered trademark of Llewellyn Worldwide Ltd.

Library of Congress Cataloging-in-Publication Data (Pending)
ISBN: 978-0-7387-7476-3

Llewellyn Worldwide Ltd. does not participate in, endorse, or have any authority or responsibility concerning private business transactions between our authors and the public.
    All mail addressed to the author is forwarded but the publisher cannot, unless specifically instructed by the author, give out an address or phone number.
    Any internet references contained in this work are current at publication time, but the publisher cannot guarantee that a specific location will continue to be maintained. Please refer to the publisher's website for links to authors' websites and other sources.

Llewellyn Publications
A Division of Llewellyn Worldwide Ltd.
2143 Wooddale Drive
Woodbury, MN 55125-2989
www.llewellyn.com

Printed in the United States of America

DEDICATION

This book is dedicated to my father, Bill Allen, who passed away while I was writing this manuscript. The rock of our family, my father taught me that I could do anything I set my mind to. Without his fervent belief in me, I don't know if I would have had the courage to pursue my dreams, one of which was writing this book. Dad, I will be eternally grateful for your love, dedication, lessons and, perhaps most of all, your laugh. I love you beyond words. What is remembered, lives.

Disclaimer

Many activities in this book use herbs and essential oils but are not to be considered anything construing medical advice. Be sure to do research on herbs, flowers, and oils before using (e.g., ingesting and applying topically) to check for toxicity, allergies and adverse reactions, and complications or interactions with any medications or conditions such as pregnancy. In addition, due to potential for fire hazard, never use anything that requires heat or a flame if you intend to sleep, *even if* the device has an auto shut-off feature.

Acknowledgments

They say it takes a village to raise a child; I believe the same is true of birthing a book. There have been so many people who have contributed to this book in some form that I probably cannot list them all but will do my best to at least provide an overview.

As always, I am grateful to my family for supporting my dreams and doing what they could to make it possible for me to bring this book to life. My husband, Richard, has spent endless hours taking care of household tasks and feeding me so that I would have the time and sustenance to write this book. He has supported my writing ambitions from the very beginning and his belief in me encouraged me to take a leap of faith in pursuing my dreams. I can't begin to thank him enough for the love and support he has given me over the past twenty years. Richard, you are my best friend, and I feel fortunate to be able to travel through life with you.

My son, Owen, has long been my biggest cheerleader and I am thankful for the many times that he has reminded me that the only limits I face are the ones I impose on myself. Owen, I am so proud of you and I love you so much! I am also blessed to have two amazing stepchildren, Emily and Steven, a son-in-law (Barrett) and a daughter-in-law (Sapida) as well as two beautiful grandchildren, Zoe and Ben, who inspire and amaze me on a daily basis.

I come from a long line of strong women, and my mother, Sandi, my sister Lisa, and my niece O'Rian are no exception. Thank you for cheering me on and reminding me of my own strength. The same goes for my cousins, Leslie and Tracy, and my Aunt Linda. My sisters-in-law Joanne, Marilyn, and Sharon have had my back from the moment I met them, and I feel blessed to be a part of their family. My friends Jackie and Stephanie continually remind me that I am a badass whenever I start to forget, and I am grateful for their love and support. A big thank you to my friend Benjamin, who pushed me to dream big when I was young.

I am, as always, immensely thankful for the Sisterhood of Avalon. The SOA has felt like home from the moment I became a sister and has enriched my life in so many ways, continually helping me to grow and evolve. My SOA sisters are some of the most amazing, inspiring women I have ever met. They have shown me the true meaning of sisterhood and I will forever be grateful. I particularly want to thank the founder of SOA, Jhenah Telyndru, for bringing such a beautiful community into existence and for her knowledge and guidance in my early stages of becoming an author.

To my friend B-One, I have so much love and gratitude for you for being in my life. You believed in me before I believed in myself and you continue to challenge me, to inspire me, and to encourage me to let go and be free. You are also the best music teacher I have ever had, and your unconditional acceptance of me means more to me than you could possibly know. Thank you for sharing with me the importance of finding the right bucket because no ordinary one will do. I am excited to see you begin to pursue your own dreams and for Chick-N-Bone to make beautiful music together!

A huge thank you to Elysia Gallo and Llewellyn for taking a chance on me and providing me with the opportunity to bring this book into being and share my ideas with the world. I am so grateful to you and I look forward to what I hope is a long-lasting collaboration.

Finally, to those dear ones who have passed before me and who continue to visit me as I sleep, including family members, friends (of the two-legged and four-legged variety), and ancestors. Both of my grandfathers and grandmothers have shared their dreams with me while alive and have visited with me after their passing. I especially want to honor my father, Bill, and my niece, Anam: I have learned so much from both of you. You are two of the most loving and pure souls I have ever met, and you continue to teach me even in death. I love you both so much and look forward to our visits in my dreams.

To anyone I may have neglected to mention by name, my deepest apologies, but please know that if you have crossed my path in any meaningful way in this life, I have learned from you and you have contributed in some way to this book and to the person I am today.

CONTENTS

ACTIVITIES

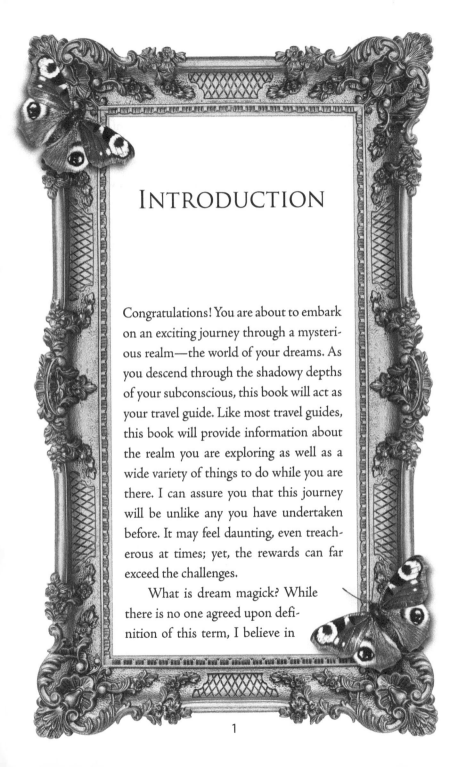

INTRODUCTION

Congratulations! You are about to embark on an exciting journey through a mysterious realm—the world of your dreams. As you descend through the shadowy depths of your subconscious, this book will act as your travel guide. Like most travel guides, this book will provide information about the realm you are exploring as well as a wide variety of things to do while you are there. I can assure you that this journey will be unlike any you have undertaken before. It may feel daunting, even treacherous at times; yet, the rewards can far exceed the challenges.

What is dream magick? While there is no one agreed upon definition of this term, I believe in its simplest terms it can be defined as using our dreams to change our reality. If we accept Aleister Crowley's definition of magick as "… the science and art of causing change to occur in conformity with will," then we may view our dreams as a tool to be used for manifesting this change.[1] Dream magick encompasses a wide range of skills which can be utilized in different ways depending on your magickal goals. This spectrum includes but is not limited to dream recall and interpretation, intuitive or prophetic dreaming, lucid dreaming, dream walking, dream projection, connection with the Underworld via dreams, healing, and dealing with nightmares.

My first experience with dream magick happened when I was just a child. I was visiting Oregon with my family and my grandfather was in the hospital. One morning, I had a very vivid dream where I was standing outside of what appeared to be a hospital when my grandfather walked over to me. He called me by the nickname he had given me and approached me wearing his usual felt fedora and a hospital gown. He giggled as he tried to hold the gown shut behind him so that he wouldn't unintentionally moon anyone. If there had been any doubt in my mind that this man was my grandfather, his goofy, childlike sense of humor confirmed that this was really him.

My grandfather told me he had to go but that he was going to be fine. He seemed to be in good spirits as he kissed the top of my head. He said he wanted to make sure that my grandmother would be okay. I noticed a black limousine parked ahead of us, from which a driver got out and told my grandfather it was time to go. My grandfather embraced me and then got into the back seat. As the car drove away, my grandfather—still grinning from ear to ear—waved goodbye. I woke up shortly thereafter, puzzled by what I had just

---

1   "Magick," Thelemapedia, updated January 21, 2022, http://www.thelemapedia.org/index.php/Magick.

seen. Before I could get out of my bed, my family members informed me that my grandfather had passed away early that morning.

My experience had been overwhelming and confusing, and I didn't know how to process it. I had been diagnosed just a few years before with a rare medical condition that among other things, made me appear physically fragile with my bone age two to three years behind my chronological age. I was also frequently ill as a child. The last thing I wanted was to give the people around me another reason to worry about me or see me as different, so I kept my dreams to myself.

Over the years, I continued to periodically have dreams that were prophetic in nature, provided answers I could not get during my waking hours, or included visits from loved ones who had passed over. Not knowing how to handle these odd occurrences, I did my best to ignore them. It wasn't until I took a psychology class in high school that I allowed myself to explore this phenomenon as a result of being required to do a research project on dreams. As part of my research, I kept a daily dream journal for several weeks.

This project turned out to be a catalyst for a lifelong passion for dream magick. Not only did I find the research on dreams intriguing, I found that when I looked back at my dream journal, I could see patterns that provided clarity and intuitive dreams that foretold later events. However, it wasn't until I was in college that I began sharing dreams with a boyfriend who validated the prophetic nature of some of my dreams involving him and told me that what I was experiencing was real. I also began to notice that other members of my family had similar dream experiences but for a variety of reasons were not able or willing to explore these experiences in depth.

Since then, I have had numerous dream experiences that have continued to benefit me in my daily life in some way, shape or form. Not all of these experiences have been joyous; in fact, some have been sad and fearsome. Yet, I have never regretted my passion for and immersion into the world of dream magick. The book that you hold in your hands is the comprehensive dream magick guide that I wish I would have had years ago when I started this journey.

Creativity and having a vivid imagination are assets in dream magick. Therefore, it's not surprising that many famous writers, musicians, and artists throughout history have experienced inspiration, prophecy, and contact with the other side through their dreams. William Blake, Charlotte Brontë, Paul McCartney, Stephen King, and Edgar Allan Poe were all known to have included some of their dream experiences in their writing, music, or films.

Dreams have also helped people to find long lost literary works. Jacopo Alighieri, son of Dante Alighieri, most famously known as the author of *The Divine Comedy*, had his father come to him in a dream to tell him where he could find the unpublished final cantos of his trilogy. Jacopo searched the house where his father had died and found the cantos in a bedroom behind a mat hanging on one the walls, just as his dream had indicated.[2] Dante's son was not the only one who had dream visitations from the other side. Samuel Clemens, better known by his pen name, Mark Twain, once stated:

> *My dream self meets friends, strangers, the dead, the living-holds both rational and irrational conversations with them upon subjects which often have not been in my waking mind—which, in some cases, could never have been it.*[3]

Sometimes inspiring or prophetic dreams have come to infamous people who would seem to be least likely to put any stock in the power of dreams. President Lincoln was said to have had a

2   Robert L. Van de Castle, *Our Dreaming Mind* (New York: Bellantine Books, 1994), 26.
3   Van de Castle, *Our Dreaming Mind*, 5–6.

dream about his own assassination two weeks before his death. Chemistry Professor Dmitri Mendeleyev created the Periodic Table of Elements in 1869 based on a dream.[4] And in 1964, the famous golfer Jack Nicklaus told a reporter at the *San Francisco Chronicle* that he had overcome a slump as a result of a dream he had wherein he was holding his golf club differently. The willingness of all of these people to take their dreams seriously and explore their potential meaning led to incredible knowledge and fascinating achievements. Imagine what these individuals and *you*, dear reader, could accomplish by harnessing the power of dreams! Yet, dream work can be challenging, frustrating, and even frightening. Dream magick requires perseverance and a willingness to be completely honest with ourselves. It requires patience and an understanding that sometimes we may unearth shadows and demons we would rather ignore.

Dream magick is a very liminal rite that differs from other types of magick in that the change that we are causing to occur in conformity with will happens while we are asleep. The activities we undertake prior to sleeping are preparation for the climax that is the magickal act, which will occur later on. Whereas other types of magickal acts or rites are undertaken while fully conscious, the culmination of our magickal working in dream magick happens while we are under the control of our subconscious.

In order to be successful, we must learn to understand the language of our subconscious, which sometimes requires being confronted with painful memories and emotions. Dreams can also be confusing and not easily interpreted. Dream magick requires a great deal of commitment and is not for the faint of heart or those expecting quick results. So why would one undertake such a challenge?

---

4 Van de Castle, *Our Dreaming Mind*, 35.

In my experience, the rewards to be gained by practicing dream magick far outweigh the drawbacks. I can point to many times in my life where I have accomplished more than I thought was possible and have avoided unnecessary pain and frustration simply by using dream magick. The rewards to be gained with dream magick include but are not limited to:

+ Creative inspiration and discovering hidden gifts
+ Effective problem-solving and the ability to see a situation clearly from a variety of angles
+ Ability to divine the future and recognize opportunities before they arise
+ Recognizing patterns that no longer serve us
+ Connection with our higher self as well as ancestors, loved ones who have passed over, deities, and guides
+ Physical, mental, and emotional healing
+ Deeply powerful and insightful shadow work
+ Manifestation
+ Greater self-knowledge
+ Clarity for making decisions and how to get "unstuck" in our personal and professional lives
+ Increased self-confidence and empowerment and deeper spiritual connections

Dream Magick is designed to help you reap all of these benefits and more. While the chapters in this book do not have to be read consecutively, I highly encourage you to read chapters 1 through 4 in succession, as they set the foundation that is critical for effective dream work.

Many people have told me that they don't dream and therefore can't do dream magick. As you will learn in chapter 1, *everyone* dreams, even if those dreams aren't remembered. Given the right tools and information, anyone can practice effective dream magick. In order to maximize the tools and information this book has to offer, you will find it helpful to approach the exercises with a playful and inquisitive open mind. Approach dream magick as an adventure rather than treating it as a chore. Don't try to rush the process and try not to get easily discouraged. I have found that when I try too hard to force a result, success eludes me and I get discouraged.

Keep in mind that most of us have spent years disregarding our dreams. In the meantime, our subconscious has been storing away thoughts, memories, and shadows and has developed a language all its own. By doing dream magick, we are developing a relationship with our subconscious and just as with any relationship it takes time and effort. Enjoy the journey itself; the results will happen. We have as much to learn from simply walking the path as we do from achieving our goals. After all, given how much we sleep we have plenty of time to practice!

It is my sincere hope that you will find the same deep satisfaction and powerful results in practicing dream magick as I have. May your courage in undertaking this journey lead you to the invaluable treasures hidden away in your subconscious. Happy dreaming!

Chapter 1
THE SCIENCE OF DREAMING

Before you start your dream work, it may be helpful to know more about the science of dreaming. Understanding when and how we dream can aid us in doing dream magick. Everyone dreams—even if we may not remember our dreams. Dreaming is universal and is a form of language which uses symbols and the ideas of the subconscious to communicate with our sleeping selves. In fact, dreaming pre-dates any known written and oral languages.

Research has validated that sleep is necessary for good health. But why do we dream? According to author Patricia Garfield, PhD, current dream researchers theorize that groups of nerve cells in our brain stem fire from time to time, and this somehow initiates the process of dreaming.[5] The theory may explain the technical "hows" of dreaming, but the purpose of dreaming appears to be multi-faceted.

Throughout our day, we are bombarded with a variety of experiences, thoughts, and input. Sensory input rarely stops, and if you consider that we are receiving feedback through not one but at least five senses, the amount of information we take in is astounding. Fortunately, our brains are able to quickly separate out the most important information in each moment in addition to what should be stored away for later or ignored altogether. Yet, we are frequently not aware of what is occurring behind the scenes; rather, much of the processing that occurs in our brains is often done automatically and swiftly and without our conscious knowledge.

Dreaming facilitates our subconscious's ability to make sense of the input we receive. It is believed that a key purpose of our dreams is to process our memories and feelings, consolidate what we have learned, and adapt our perspectives based on new information. Experiences, thoughts, or emotions we may have forgotten about on a conscious level may still be lurking in our subconscious, calling out for attention in our dreams. While we may think we are done with them, if we have not fully processed or healed from them, they may not be done with us. I have found this to be particularly true if these experiences involve trauma in any way.

In addition to our brain stem's nerve cells, the pineal gland plays a critical role in dreaming. The pineal gland sits in the middle of our brain and is often associated with our third eye, the space between our eyebrows. The pineal gland responds to changing light levels and releases the hormone melatonin, which helps us to not only fall

---

5   Patricia Garfield, *Creative Dreaming: Plan and Control Your Dreams to Develop Creativity, Overcome Fears, Solve Problems, and Create a Better Self* (New York: Simon and Schuster, 1995), 34.

asleep but also regulates our circadian rhythms—the physical, mental, and behavioral changes that follow a 24-hour cycle.[6] The pineal gland produces the chemicals DMT and pinoline, which are responsible for causing dream states and visions as well as stimulating the imagination. The pineal gland is connected to our metabolism and enables us to shift into different levels of consciousness.[7]

Dreaming also assists with learning and memory, and plays an important role in obtaining and assimilating new information and skills. Dan Margoliash, professor of biology at the University of Chicago attests:

> A lot of scientists I know are also musicians and they frequently have the experience of practicing a difficult new musical piece and not getting it down, but when they come back to it after a couple of nights sleep, they suddenly have it, even without practicing in the meantime.[8]

As noted in the introduction, many famous artists, writers, musicians, actors, and even scientists have stated that some of their greatest accomplishments had origins in one or more of their dreams. It would seem plausible that there may be a connection between the act of dreaming and the act of creating. In fact, many of the people I have met or read about who have had profound success with dream magick have been individuals with a strong sense of curiosity, creativity, and a vivid imagination. When dream magick practitioners describe their dreams, it is not uncommon for them to state that the dream felt incredibly real. I, too, have had dreams

---

6   "Pineal Gland," Cleveland Clinic website, last updated June 22, 2022, https:// my.clevelandclinic.org/health/body/23334-pineal-gland.

7   Nimue Brown, *Pagan Dreaming: The Magic of Altered Consciousness* (Winchester, UK: Moon Books, 2015), 25.

8   Andrea Rock, *The Mind At Night: The New Science of How and Why We Dream* (New York: Basic Books, 2005), 93.

that felt real and it appears that there may be scientific validity for this experience. Stephen LaBerge is perhaps one of the most prominent individuals in the world of dream studies and has written many books on lucid dreaming in addition to founding the Lucidity Institute. As LaBerge points out, "the physiological effects in the brain and body of dream activities are nearly identical to the effects of experience in waking life."[9]

While there is no research that decisively shows that dreaming is vital to our survival, many scientists believe that dreaming plays an important role in our physical and mental health, especially as it relates to tasks such as integrating memories, emotionally processing daily events, and stimulating problem-solving and creativity.

DREAMS AFFECTED BY PHYSICAL AND MENTAL CONDITIONS

The critical roles that sleeping and dreaming play in our overall physical and mental health have led to some interesting studies about how some disabilities and brain trauma affect the dreaming experience. Dreaming seems like such a visual experience, and I have often wondered what the dreaming process might be like for someone who is visually impaired. Psychologist Nancy Kerr's studies help to shed some light on this topic. Kerr's studies showed that individuals who became blind before the age of five rarely experienced visual imagery in their dreams.[10] Dr. Christopher Baird asserts that visually impaired dreamers dream more often in sounds, smells, and touch.

Individuals who lost their sight between the ages of five and seven sometimes retained their visual dreams, but those who became blind after the age of seven dreamed in much the same way that non-visually-impaired adults would. It would therefore seem that

9   Stephen LaBerge, *Lucid Dreaming: A Concise Guide to Awakening in Your Dreams and in Your Life* (Boulder, CO: Sounds True Publishing, 2009), 15.

10   Rock, *The Mind At Night*, 36.

dreaming is not solely about what we see—it can include things like how we feel and how we think about other things or people when those things or people are not around. These studies make it clear that dream magick is accessible to most of us, despite any perceived physical limitations we may have.

Research on sighted individuals who had experienced some sort of brain trauma (such as lesions) is also intriguing. A psychologist named Allan Hobson conducted studies and learned that some patients with brain lesions continually dream—in fact, they can't stop dreaming, even when awake. The research also found that persons who had experienced damage to a specific set of cells in the base of the brain typically had very vivid dreams. These individuals also had a difficult time differentiating between what was a dream and what was a real event.[11]

Mental health conditions such as depression or anxiety can also affect a person's dreaming process. Studies indicate that the problem-solving area of the brain in someone with a diagnosis of depression typically never shuts down during dreaming. As a result, sleep—particularly the Rapid Eye Movement (REM) phase of sleep—is not as effective in regenerating or healing the body and mind. Andrea Rock, science journalist and author of *The Mind At Night*, writes that "some psychologists suggest a properly functioning dreaming system may actually be more effective than some forms of psychotherapy."[12]

STAGES OF SLEEP

In order to determine the best way to induce lucid or prophetic dreaming, we must understand the stages of sleep that the average individual experiences leading into vital REM sleep. They are as follows:

---

11 Rock, *The Mind At Night*, 47.
12 Rock, *The Mind At Night*, 112.

Pre-Sleep: This is the time right before we fall asleep when we are relaxed and start tuning out sounds and possible distractions. During this stage, the brain makes alpha waves that are similar to when we are in deep thought or meditation.

Stage One: This stage consists of some visual imagery but it's typically fleeting as the brain and body are just settling into sleep. Visual imagery that does occur generally features imagery related to events of the day.

Stage Two: Light sleep occurs in this stage. Our brain makes large, slow delta waves lasting less than a half hour.

Stage Three: Delta waves continue in this stage, which lasts for roughly fifteen to thirty minutes before moving into REM sleep. This stage is when sleepwalking is most likely to occur.

REM Sleep: In this stage, brain activity increases in short yet fast patterns that look the same as if one was experiencing waking activity.

Psychophysiologist and lucid dream researcher Stephen LaBerge posits that there are two kinds of sleep: an idle, restorative sleep known as "quiet sleep," and REM sleep, associated with rapid eye movements, twitching, a very active brain, and feelings of paralysis. As LaBerge points out, while REM isn't the only stage of sleep that produces dreams, it is a stage in which we have a "switched on brain in a switched off body."[13] The initial cycle from pre-sleep to REM sleep takes about an hour or so with REM sleep consisting of roughly an hour at first. As the sleep cycles continue, REM sleep starts to last longer.

It is during REM sleep that our brain chemistry changes and allows us to have dream experiences that are not limited by our waking experiences of what is possible. These dream experiences can

---

13   LaBerge, *Lucid Dreaming*, 15.

include being in two places at once, being able to perform actions that we can't in our waking life, and experiencing a dream from more than one perspective. Whereas the sensory input we receive in our daily life comes from outside of ourselves, the sensory stimuli in our dreams is completely internally initiated. It may be that having a vivid imagination and an open mind lends itself to fewer dream limitations, which could be why so many artists have attested to having dreams that were a breakthrough and what led them to create an amazing work of art.

The types of dreams we are most likely to have depend on the sleep stage we are in. In the REM state, dreams tend to be more dramatic and can play out like an action, thriller, or horror movie. Non-REM sleep states are typically comprised of dreams that are a bit calmer, more introspective, and similar to watching a documentary.[14] PET scans of dreamers have shown that the brain is generally more active in REM sleep compared not only to other stages of sleep but also the brain's activity in our waking lives.

Dream researchers typically agree that it is during REM sleep that we are most likely to experience lucid dreaming. Specifically, the last two phases of REM sleep (typically during early morning hours or the hours right before we awaken) are the most conducive to lucid dreaming.[15] The additional advantage with the last phases of REM sleep is that because these dreams take place closer to when we awaken, we are more likely to remember them.

However, this is not to say that we can't do dream magick during non-REM sleep states. The theta sleep state occurs shortly in the liminal space between being awake and being fully asleep. During this time period, we tend to be somewhat conscious but our

---

14   Garfield, *Creative Dreaming*, 35.
15   Dylan Tucciillo, Jared Zeizel, and Thomas Peisel, *A Field Guide to Lucid Dreaming* (New York: Workman Publishing, 2013), 101–02.

body is fully relaxed. While the dreams in theta sleep may not be as vivid or full of action, this is a powerful state for dream manifestation. Scientists have found that during Theta sleep we are more susceptible to programming and suggestion.[16] We can take advantage of Theta sleep by immersing ourselves in visualizing and thinking about that which we wish to dream about. The more real we can make our thoughts and visualizations, the more likely that we can write the script to some extent for our dreams and by doing so forge a connection between our conscious and our subconscious.

Dreams are a liminal state that provide a laboratory of sorts in which we can gather information, speak with those no longer on our plane or in close physical proximity, obtain insights that we might not be able to access in the waking world, foretell the future, process our trauma, and experience what would normally be impossible in the waking world. The limitations of our waking world are not a feature of our dreamscapes.

The dream world allows us to practice magick on a level that we either may not be able to or may not be confident enough to attempt in the waking world. Dreaming activates and hones our imagination and creativity and facilitates nonlinear thinking that can help us form associations and achieve realizations that we wouldn't otherwise achieve. Perhaps most powerfully, through dreams we can make our subconscious an active ally rather than something that simply lurks in the background, affecting our lives in ways that our conscious mind doesn't fully recognize or understand. As author James Hillman points out, "Dreaming is the psyche itself doing its soul-work."[17]

---

16   Joe Dispenza, *Evolve Your Brain: The Science of Changing Your Mind* (Deerfield Beach, FL: Health Communications, 2007), 464–65.

17   Edward Tick, *The Practice of Dream Healing* (Wheaton, IL: Quest Books, 2001), 36.

Chapter 2

DREAMS ACROSS CULTURES AND TIMES

Since time immemorial, cultures all over the world have alternately feared, revered, and tried to understand the stories that played out in their heads as they lie sleeping. All humans need sleep, and all humans dream, yet the purpose of dreaming is still somewhat mysterious. Given this and given that the body is in a liminal state when we dream, it is not surprising that the vast majority of cultures associate dreams with the Divine.

DREAMS IN ANCIENT AND INDIGENOUS CULTURES

While we can't know for sure when and where dreams began to be analyzed, we do know that the

Babylonians were the first to record their dreams on stone tablets dating to around 3100 BCE.[18]

Dreams have made an appearance in a variety of religious documents and stories. Both the Bible and the Koran have stories of prophetic dreams. The ancient Mesopotomian *Epic of Gilgamesh* also references dream and dream interpretations. Compiled around 2100 BCE, it describes Gilgamesh having a dream about a meteor falling to Earth that is interpreted by the goddess Ninsun to mean that a close friend would arrive soon.[19]

Mesopotamian cultures believed dreams could be predictive and took them very seriously. There were professional dream interpreters and interpretations of dreams were recorded in what is known as the "Assyrian Dream Book."[20] In a sixteenth-century dream interpretation book, a Chinese philosopher asked how we truly know whether we are asleep or awake.[21]

Ancient Egyptians paid close attention to their dreams as they believed that their dreams were associated with and could come from both the Divine and the deceased. Ramesses II wrote a dream interpretation book on papyrus at some point between 1279 and 1213 BCE.[22] The famous collection also known as the Chester Beatty papyri, believed to be written between 1991 to 1786 BCE,

---

18   Juliette den Hollander, "History of Dream Research," Sutori website, (n.d.), https://www.sutori.com/en/story/the-history-of-dream-research-aHZ2EkuAQtRJgjhMMjxJ7bvX.

19   Indlieb Farazi Saber, "While you were sleeping: The importance of dreams in Middle Eastern culture," Middle East Eye website, November 16, 2021, https://www.middleeasteye.net/discover/dreams-middle-east-civilisation-how-helped-define.

20   Mingren Wu, "Oneiromancy: Dream Predictions in Ancient Mesopotomia," Ancient Origins website, March 17, 2020, https://www.ancient-origins.net/history-ancient-traditions/oneiromancy-and-dream-predictions-ancient-mesopotamia-005726.

21   "History of Dream Interpretation", Oniri website, August 10, 2022, https://www.oniri.io/post/a-bit-of-history-of-dream-interpretation#:~:text=Humans%20have%20tried%20to%20interpret,symbolic%20dreams%20through%20different%20rituals.

22   Saber, "While you were sleeping."

also contains methods for interpreting dreams. Muslim Sufis practiced a form of dream incubation as well as lucid dreaming as noted by twelfth-century Sufi philosopher Idn Arabi.[23] The earliest Middle Eastern dream book still in existence was written by Persian scholar Ibn Qutaybah in the ninth century.[24]

Indigenous peoples also have a long history of reverence for dreams. While each tribe has its own unique way of looking at dreams, there have been commonalities documented across indigenous cultures. These commonalities include dreams as givers of prophecy and powers, a belief that dreams are future-oriented rather than reflections of the past, and that they are important events often with great spiritual and personal meaning. Dreams are generally viewed as powerful, and often the line between what constitutes a dream versus a vision is blurred.

The culture of the Mohave people was strongly influenced by dreams as they believed that dreams had the power to cure illnesses.[25] Some peoples, such as the Australian Aborigines, believed that the world was brought into being through dreams and that dreams are "...the sign of the soul wandering around the world during sleep."[26] The Jivaro tribe in Ecuador believes that in order to be successful in hunting and war, they must have an *arutam*, or soul that is only provided to them via dreams.[27] Traditional Plains people do not view dreams as messages from the unconscious; rather, they see

23   Saber, "While you were sleeping."
24   Saber, "While you were sleeping."
25   "History of Dream Interpretation," Oniri website.
26   "History of Dream Interpretation," Oniri website.
27   Waud H. Kracke, "Cultural Aspects of Dreaming," International Institute for Dream Research, https://www.dreamresearch.ca/pdf/cultural.pdf.

them as coming directly from dream spirits who share information with the dreamer to help them be successful.[28]

The Peruvian Amazon tribe called the Sonenekuinaji ascribe to a dream reality that they call *eshawa* in which the lines between dreams and waking reality are blurred and all creatures, beings and animate objects are interconnected.[29] The tribe also used to dreams to find food and medicinal herbs and name their children. According to author and documentary editor Katharine Asals, the Iroquois, "…are a people with a highly elaborate and complex dreaming culture."[30] Their strong belief in dreams as oracles and what they call "masters" has led them to view dreams as edicts that must be carried out. In addition, the Iroquois were known to incorporate dream healing and a dream "guessing game" into their Midwinter Festival. During the guessing game, people would share clues about a specific dream they had and the other participants had to accurately guess what the dream was about.[31]

ANCIENT GREECE

Perhaps the most extensive record that we have regarding the role dreams played in the lives of individuals and society in general come from the ancient Greeks. When we look at the stories and historical artifacts from ancient Greece, it becomes apparent that dreams were important to the lives of everyone, regardless of socioeconomic status. Author Dr. Edward Tick asserts that "in the ancient world, dreams were not shadow plays … Rather, dreaming was a primary

28   Katharine Asals, "Chapter 2–Dream Theory in Native North America," Katharine Asals website, https://katharineasals.com/articles/the-trope-of-the-dream-and-other-irrational-moments/chapter-2-dream-theory-in-native-north-america/.

29   Alessandro Casale, "Indigenous Dreams: Prophetic Nature, Spirituality, and Survivance," Indigenous New Hampshire Collaborative Collective website, accessed 8/28/23, https://indigenousnh.com/2019/01/25/indigenous-dreams/.

30   Asals, "Chapter 2."

31   Asals, "Chapter 2."

activity of the soul. Dream stories were events that occurred to the soul in a living, otherworldly dimension."[32]

In the ancient world, dreams were often taken as literal messages and as actual events that occurred in the realm of the soul. Dreams were viewed as important, and the ancient Greeks saw dreams as providing them with a direct connection to the Divine. As a result, they built more than three hundred shrines and dream temples. They even had deities that presided over the dream realm. Many of the deities seen as dream allies are also associated with liminal states and the Underworld. This is not surprising when you consider the stillness of our bodies while we are sleeping and the fact that sleep itself was once called "the little death." (A listing of dream ally deities can be found in appendix B).

Hypnos was one of the deities associated with dreaming, and it is from his name that we get the term "hypnosis." Hypnos was the Greek god of sleep who was said to have lived in Erebos, a realm known for its never-ending darkness. Hypnos was the son of the Greek goddess Nyx and had a twin brother named Thanatos, whose name means "peaceful death." The oneiroi, beings who brought dreams to humans, were said to be either his siblings or his children.[33] Hypnos's son Morpheus, the god of dreaming, led the oneiroi but could only influence the dreams of other gods and nobles.[34]

Unlike some cultures, in ancient Greece people generally believed that anyone could communicate with the gods in their dreams. Perhaps this is why dream incubation played a critical role in Greek society. People would travel all over to visit famous shrines and temples

---

32 Tick, *Dream Healing*, xix.

33 Kenn Payne, "Hypnos," in Naming the God, ed. Trevor Greenfield (Winchester, UK: Moon Books, 2022), 154.

34 Bethany Williams, "Morpheus: The Greek God of Dreams and Nightmares," The Collector website, March 17, 2022, https://www.thecollector.com/morpheus-greek-god/.

such as Delphi to undertake dream incubation to seek answers to questions, obtain healing advice, and communicate with their ancestors. Delphi was a travel destination for thousands of Greeks who sought answers, a great deal of which were related to physical ailments.

The Necromanteion, also known as the "Oracle of the Dead," is near the River Acheron in Epirus, near the ancient city of Ephyra. The Necromanteion was associated with the Greek deities Hades and Persephone. As such, it was believed to be connected to the Underworld. The Necromanteion consisted of winding underground corridors lit only by torches. These dark, maze-like corridors were intended to mimic the journey into the Underworld. While some querents went through ritual process during their waking hours to seek messages from those who had passed, there were some who practiced dream incubation and thus slept in the corridors overnight in hopes of a visitation from a deceased loved one or ancestor.

Dreams as a Healing Modality

Perhaps the most well-known Greek dream incubation temples were those dedicated to Asklepios. Considered to be the son of Apollo, Asklepios was known for his skill in medicine and healing As the myth goes, Apollo, god of medicine and prophecy (among other things), was involved with Koronis, the princess of Thessaly. When Apollo learned that Koronis had gotten pregnant by another man, he sent his twin sister, Artemis, to kill Koronis. The child was pulled out of its mother's corpse and named Asklepios before being turned over to Chiron, a centaur well-versed in the healing arts.

Chiron passed all of his knowledge of herbs and healing to Asklepios, who went on to also learn what we would call psychotherapy in this day and age. Apollo was said to have passed on his gifts of diagnosis, healing, and insight to Asklepios. Impressed with Asklepios, Athena also gave him healing powers in the form of the blood of Medusa. According to myths, the blood from the right side of Medusa's body was known to heal whereas the blood of her left side had the power to kill. Despite having all of this knowledge and power, Asklepios soon found himself at odds with Hades as a result of using his power to bring back the dead. Hades complained to Zeus, who was persuaded to agree that no mortal should have that much power and killed Asklepios with his thunderbolt. However, after reconsidering Asklepios's talent, Zeus eventually made him a god of healing and allowed him to return to the land of the living. Asklepios is best known for his symbol, a staff with a snake wrapped around it.

Greek scholar Dr. Edward Tick states that Asklepios would visit the dreamer in his normal form or in his animal form as a snake or dog. There were various procedures involved in dream incubation, as we will discover in chapter 9. In the case of one of Asklepios's temples, the cure for one's ailment(s) would often happen through the apparition of the god. However, there were other ways or instructions for dreamers to obtain healing. For example, Dr. Tick shares that one temple provided this "prescription" for healing: "…after fasting for three days, the supplicant should immerse himself in the pool of Parthenius, though it be winter, and pray to Artemis—the healing would come."[35]

Other seekers claimed to have experienced "dream surgery" at one of the temples; as they were dreaming, they would see a deity performing a medical procedure on the area of their body that was ailing. These seekers claim to have been cured upon awakening. Asklepios and his cults were known beyond Greece. Pergamum in

---

35   Tick, *Dream Healing*, xiv.

Turkey was the site of a shrine to Asklepios that was taken over by Rome in 129 BCE. As popular as Asklepios's temples were, the spread of Christianity eventually wiped out the many cults and temples devoted to Asklepios or, in some cases, caused devotees to hide their practices. Asklepios's cult endured in Greece until roughly the fifth century CE.[36]

MODERN PSYCHOLOGY OF DREAMS

The two figures that are likely the most associated with dream research in modern history are psychologists Sigmund Freud and Carl Jung. Sigmund Freud brought dreams back into the public eye in the late 1800s when he published his book, *The Interpretation of Dreams*. Freud believed that dreams helped us understand what was occurring in our waking lives, though he centered his theories on what he saw as the repressed desires, often of a sexual or aggressive nature. According to Freud, the content of dreams is derived from physical stimulus while we are asleep (i.e., the urge to urinate), things that occurred the previous day, and things that happened when we were very young that our conscious mind does not remember.[37]

Freud believed that the latent content of dreams came about as a result of our attempts to bury desires considered taboo and unacceptable by society. Of course, given our subconscious's penchant for symbolism and ambiguity, the dreamer often cannot make sense of the messages the subconscious is trying to convey. Freud therefore prescribed free association as a way to understand the latent meaning of our dreams. In theory, a psychoanalyst could listen to the

---

36   Tick, *Dream Healing*, xiv.
37   Emily Rodriguez, "Oneiromancy," Britannica website, updated April 16, 2016, https://www.britannica.com/topic/oneiromancy.

dreamer's free associations and help them understand their hidden desires and overcome inhibitions.

Carl Jung was originally a student of Freud's, but his view of dreams differed greatly from that of his mentor. Whereas Freud saw the subconscious trying to hide things from the dreamer, Jung believed that dreams were an attempt by the subconscious to share what had been hidden and provide insights into one's psyche. Jung focused on the interaction in dreams between ourselves (as represented by our "dream ego") and other dream figures. An added element to Jung's theories was the belief in archetypes, which were formed by what he called the "collective unconscious," a portion of our subconscious that consisted of ancestral memories that were passed down from generation to generation.[38]

The purpose of the collective unconscious, according to Jung, was so that we could tap into helpful information during a crisis. Jung's dream theories were of a dual nature, in that he believed that similar archetypes could be found across numerous diverse cultures, thus making some portion of what they represent in our dreams universal in their symbolism. At the same time, because our subconscious minds are unique to us, our dreams can only be understood through knowledge of the individual dreamer. Jung's most famous writing on the subject—*Memories, Dreams, Reflections, Man and His Symbols*, and *Dreams*—expound on his theories.

With the progression of modern technology, there have been great advancements in dream research, especially as it relates to lucid dreaming. One of the most prominent is the "continuity hypothesis," which asserts that there is "…a continuity in mental functioning

---

38   Lisa Fritscher, "Carl Jung's Collective Unconscious Theory: What It Says About the Mind," VeryWellMind website, May 17 2023, https://www.verywellmind.com/what-is -the-collective-unconscious-2671571.

from waking life to sleep."[39] Dream research has expanded a great deal to include studies on specific challenges or experiences such as how to help individuals with Post Traumatic Stress Disorder (PTSD) deal with ongoing nightmares.

---

39   Christian Roesler, "Jungian theory of dreaming and contemporary dream research – findings from the research project 'Structural Dream Analysis,'" *Analytical Psychology* 65, no. 1 (February 2020): 44–62, DOI: 10.1111/1468-5922.12566.

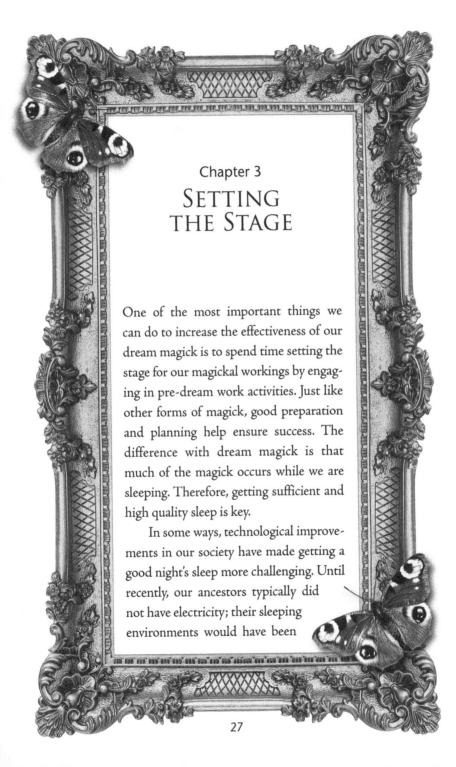

Chapter 3
SETTING THE STAGE

One of the most important things we can do to increase the effectiveness of our dream magick is to spend time setting the stage for our magickal workings by engaging in pre-dream work activities. Just like other forms of magick, good preparation and planning help ensure success. The difference with dream magick is that much of the magick occurs while we are sleeping. Therefore, getting sufficient and high quality sleep is key.

In some ways, technological improvements in our society have made getting a good night's sleep more challenging. Until recently, our ancestors typically did not have electricity; their sleeping environments would have been much darker, and sleeping patterns were more naturally aligned with the time of day as opposed to being artificially determined. Technological advancements have resulted in inventions such as televisions, smartphones, and laptops, which provide us with entertainment, social connection, and access to information. However, many studies have shown that the blue light that emits from these devices actually block production of the sleep hormone, melatonin, thus making it more difficult for us to fall into a restful sleep.

There are many other factors that can affect our quality of sleep. Some of these are natural and could have affected ancient cultures, but most are modern problems. These factors include but are not limited to the following:

+ Stress levels
+ Hormonal changes
+ Moon phases
+ Artificial light
+ Work schedules
+ Sound disruptions
+ Illness
+ Effects of modern medication, recreational drugs, and alcohol
+ Bed sharing

Sleep challenges have been on the rise for many years, and the COVID-19 pandemic has drastically negatively impacted our quality and quantity of sleep. According to an article published by the American Psychological Association, as of 2021 two out of every three Americans reported that they were experiencing either insomnia or a tendency to sleep too much.[40]

---

40 Zara Abrams, "Growing Concerns About Sleep," *American Psychological Association* 40, no. 4 (2021): https://www.apa.org/monitor/2021/06/news-concerns-sleep.

Laying the Groundwork

The first step in preparing for dream work is to do everything we can to lay the groundwork for a peaceful sleep experience. There are many practical steps we can take to accomplish this goal. Using blackout curtains and a sleep mask can help block out light that could interfere with sleep. Avoiding blue light two to three hours before falling asleep is also very helpful. (If you must use tools that emit blue light shortly before going to bed, you can purchase blue light blocking glasses.) If you cannot remove any sound distractions that could impede your sleep, you may want to try playing white noise to minimize the impacts of sounds.

Sharing a bed with another person or a beloved pet can also influence our sleep patterns. If possible, you may want to remove your pets from your bedroom on the nights you are doing dream magick or sleep in another room. (More information about creating your own dream temple is provided in chapter 9).

It is also important to avoid alcohol and other substances prior to doing dream magick. It may sound counterintuitive, as some substances are known to have a relaxing effect. However, substances such as marijuana can be relaxing but for some reason often seem to disrupt one's sleep patterns and quality of dreams, and various studies have also shown that marijuana can suppress REM sleep.

Some people also refrain from eating meat, sugar, and caffeine prior to undertaking dream magick. I have found that I am better able to focus in rituals and magickal acts in general when I don't consume these items for at least three to four hours prior to undertaking magick. My body can sometimes feel heavier when I consume these things, and caffeine can make it hard to get into a restful state. This is a personal choice, of course, but I would encourage you to try refraining from these items when doing dream work to see if it makes a difference. Eating too much of anything prior to going to bed for the evening can also disrupt sleep.

Studies have also found that allowing for wind-down time prior to sleep can be helpful in dream work efforts. According to Dr. Patricia Garfield, author of *Creative Dreaming*, numerous studies have shown that when a person spends time alone in quiet, restful activities prior to sleep, they are more likely to be aware of their dreams and have longer cycles of REM sleep by as much as 60 percent as compared to those who do not partake in peaceful, solitary activities.[41] I have personally found that incorporating some sort of ritual or "trigger" when doing pre-dream work activities can, over time, make it easier to shift my mindset into one more aligned with and focused on intentional dreaming. As one example, I used to have a difficult time getting my mind to shut off whether I was attempting meditation or dream work; my brain seemed to jump from one thought to the other, and I had a hard time staying focused and still. Over time, however, I found that by lighting incense prior to beginning these activities, my brain began to understand the incense smell as a cue to settle down, and now my ability to get into a dream readiness state happens more quickly and easily through this one simple act.

ACCESSING THE WORLD OF THE LIMINAL

Many world myths and indigenous practices related to rituals, connection to the Divine, and accessing a liminal state point to the necessity of purification and removal from the mundane as a precursor to undertaking magickal work. I find this to be particularly applicable when it comes to dream work. Various myths and traditions point to the utilization of certain plants and oils that can act as

---

41   Garfield, *Creative Dreaming*, 92.

allies in purification and removal from the mundane. These include but are not limited to:[42]

+ Sleeping under a plant ally,

+ Putting herbs such as yarrow, plantain, burdock, and mugwort in a dream pillow, the latter of these said to assist in having dreams of a future spouse. Mugwort root in general was believed to be an effective dream amulet,

+ Making an infusion of brandy or vodka with dream-aligned, nontoxic plants and either drinking some of the tincture or anointing oneself with it,

+ Using decoctions of mugwort, rose, orange blossom, and or magnolia in a bath to induce dreams,

+ Burning nontoxic dream-aligned plants as incense, and

+ Chanting things in threes

More information about dream work aligned herbs and oils can be found in appendix C.

DREAM ALLIES

Dream allies are entities who can assist you in your magickal efforts. Allies can be deities, animals, mythical creatures, or even plants. You may find that a deity you are already working with may be helpful in your dream work as well. Many deities and other entities aligned with psychopomp (guides for the souls of the dead) activities and the Underworld can also make great dream allies because of the liminality of both realms. Appendix B offers a comprehensive list of potential dream allies, but you can also find your personal dream allies using the guided meditation that follows. If you are just starting

---

42 Corinne Boyer, *Dream Divination Plants in the Northern European Tradition* (Hercules, CA: Three Hands Press, 2022), 23, 26, 44, 59–61, 85.

your exploration into dream magick, you may wish to ask for a general dream ally to work with. However, you can also use this meditation to meet dream allies to work with you on a specific purpose such as lucid dreaming or contacting your ancestors in dreams. I highly encourage you to journal about this experience or at the very least draw a picture of or otherwise describe the symbol and any pertinent information you were given. As time goes by, it can be easy to forget what you've been told in the astral realm, and you might even find that information given to you in the meditation that may not seem meaningful will prove to be pertinent and make more sense as your dream magick efforts evolve.

Meeting Your Dream Allies

Sit or lie in a comfortable position in a space where you are not likely to be interrupted. Start by taking several deep, slow breaths in and out. When you feel sufficiently relaxed, visualize a door in front of you. This can be any type of door-even a portal. When you are ready, step through the doorway and find yourself in a forest clearing at night. Although it is dark, the stars and the full moon above provide enough light for you to see what is in front of you and around you.

In the middle of the clearing is a large oak tree in full bloom, its branches reaching out in all different directions, while a gentle breeze causes the leaves of the tree to sway back and forth in an almost hypnotic dance. At the base of the oak tree is a beautiful bowl that you come to realize is for offerings. You sit for a moment facing the tree as you think about what it is you wish to accomplish with your dream work. When you are ready, you state your desire to find a dream ally as you leave an offering of some kind in the bowl. You then walk a short distance from the tree and sit on the ground facing the large oak.

Upon sitting, you close your eyes and concentrate on the information you are receiving from your other senses as you wait for your dream ally (or allies) to approach. Soon you feel a charge of energy in the air as you hear a rustling sound near the tree. Take a moment to notice any changes that your senses have picked up on. What sounds do you hear? Is there an identifiable smell that you can pick up? What does the energy around you now feel like? After you have taken a moment to immerse yourself in these sensory inputs, open your eyes. There, positioned by the oak tree, is your dream ally.

Your dream ally moves toward you and settles down directly across from you. Your ally then begins to communicate with you. It could be through a human-sounding voice, an animal-like noise, or even thoughts or pictures that arise in your mind. Whichever form of communication your ally uses, you will intuitively understand what they are trying to say. They ask you why you have requested their presence and what assistance you wish for. You take a moment to respond to their questions. You then listen to any information they may have to share with you. You ask by what name you shall call them, and they respond.

When your ally has finished sharing information with you, they ask you to hold out your hand so that they may give you a symbol that will act as a key should you need to contact them again in the astral realm or wish to invoke them during your dream magick efforts. Pay close attention to the symbol you are given, as you will use it to connect with them in the future. You can use this symbol by visualizing it or drawing it in ritual and in your dreams. Should you wish to converse with your dream ally for deeper understanding of your dreams and to receive guidance about your dream work, you need only to

*return to this space and place the symbol in the oak tree and
your ally will reappear.*

*When you are ready, thank your ally and turn to leave.
Walk back to the clearing and see a path leading through the forest to the door into this realm. Walk through the door and return
to mundane reality, taking several deep breaths and touching
your hands to the ground if needed. When you are ready, open
your eyes.*

CREATING A SAFE SPACE

Throughout the rest of this chapter are several activities designed
to help you set the stage for dream work. As with most types of
magickal undertaking, it is important to ensure that the space in
which you will be dreaming is protected both in the mundane sense
(i.e., from potential disruptions) and in a magickal sense. I make sure
to do some sort of warding or casting of sacred space prior to doing
any dream work activities. Safe space can be created in many different ways, including but not limited to casting a circle, using Reiki
or other magickal symbols to purify and protect space, and invok-
ing dream work-aligned deities and allies and asking them to stand
guard at the corners and entrances of your room for protection.

Warding

This practice is best done prior to dream work activities and going
to sleep. Here are the basic steps:

1. Purify your space. This can be done in a variety of ways
    such as walking around the physical space while using
    musical instruments (e.g., bells, crystal singing bowls,
    drums, or vocal tones), asperging the area with moon
    or other sacred water, and using sacred herbs known for

purification. (Note: White sage and palo santo are used by indigenous peoples as part of cultural practices, so it is strongly recommended that you avoid using these herbs; white sage in particular is also threatened by overharvesting. Other common herbs such as garden sage, lavender, mugwort, and rosemary can be used just as effectively for purification purposes. Be sure to do your research if you are not sure if an herb you are planning on using is associated with an indigenous culture that is not your own or if it is at risk of being overharvested).

2. Set your intention. I typically vocalize my intention for creating sacred, protected space, most often stating it three times.

3. Cast a circle. This is optional but can add a layer of intention to your warding efforts. When casting a circle for these purposes, I like to envision a protective outer ring around the perimeters of my room such as a circle of standing stones, a wall of fire, or a transparent sheet of ice. Your vision for your circle is limited only by your imagination.

4. Choose your tools, allies, and symbols that you will use to act as protective wards. If I am working with a deity or dream ally, I will often do a guided journey to meet with them and politely ask for their assistance. I will also listen to any feedback they share with me, as they sometimes have helpful suggestions or potential pitfalls to watch out for. I will then envision my allies and deities stationed at each corner and entrance to the room. If you are working only with one specific ally, you can envision duplicates of them at each corner and access point. If you are working with multiple allies or deities, you may want to consider

where they should be stationed based on factors such as elemental and directional associations.

You can also use physical items in conjunction with these allies or on their own. These physical items can include rocks or crystals, spiritual tools, herbs, and other physical symbolic representations of protection and allies. When using physical items, I place them in each of the corners and access points to my room.

5. When you are done with your dream work, take down the circle and wards. I personally find it effective to take down the circle and wards the next day after I wake and do so because it further distinguishes the mundane purpose of my room when I am not doing magick from when I am intentionally practicing my craft. You could certainly leave circle and wards in place, but they must be strengthened and maintained on a regular basis in order to be effective.

DREAM ALTARS

Another powerful component of dream magick is the creation of a dream altar. A dream altar is much like any other altar used in magick, a focal point for magickal workings. Altars help us connect with the Divine and magickal energies associated with what it is we wish to accomplish. There really are no specific requirements for how big an altar must be or what should be placed on it, so you can be creative when putting your altar together.

If you have the space in your home, you may wish to construct an altar on any number of surfaces such as a shelf, a dresser, a fireplace mantle, or a small table. (Altars can also be made outside but unless you are planning on doing your dream work outdoors, an outside altar would likely not be as effective for dream magick). If you do not have space in which to construct a mid- to large-sized altar or do not want to draw attention to your workings, you can also use items such as a small box or tin. I have found cigar boxes and books that are actually boxes to be sufficient. You can find small tins at local craft stores or use a tin that used to contain mints.

As with any altar, you will want to incorporate items that correspond to your intent. This could include dream-aligned crystals or herbs, representations of the moon and stars, and elemental representations such as for air or water. If you have a specific focus for your dreaming, you can include a symbol for that as well. For example, if you wish to dream about relationship matters, you could place a heart on your dream altar. If your intent is to connect with a deceased loved one, a picture of that person and something that was important to them can be used. Dream sachets, pillows, and dolls can also be placed on the altar. I recommend dusting your altar if possible on a regular basis and perhaps even leaving offerings there from time to time.

My dream altar changes from time to time but typically includes many of the following:

- A candle or fairy lights (to represent the stars in the sky)
- Crystals such as amethysts, moonstone, gold stone, and dendritic agate
- Roses, lavender, and mugwort
- A small chalice of moon water, fresh spring water, or water from a natural source such as a river or ocean (Water has long been connected with liminal states and journeys to worlds outside of our mundane realm)
- An incense burner and incense
- A feather (to represent the "flight" that occurs when we are dreaming)

+ A dream doll or pillow
+ A scrying bowl or mirror
+ A bell I ring prior to doing dream magick to denote that I am moving into a liminal and magickal state
+ Symbols of dream guides or deities such as a small owl figurine and a small statue of Persephone (A comprehensive list of dream-aligned deities and guides can be found in appendix B)
+ Tarot or oracle cards associated with my dream intentions
+ Silver yarn to connect me to Arianrhod and the world of dreams

I have also used travel dream altars in small tins that held items that were not overtly magickal. They included things like a small flameless candle, a crystal, a blue or silver string, and a dream-related sigil or rune drawn on a small piece of paper. When traveling, I simply place the container on my nightstand and look at it while visualizing my dream intentions shortly before going to bed.

CRAFTING DREAM DOLLS AND SACHETS

Dream dolls and dream pillows or sachets can be quite helpful in dream work efforts, and fortunately you don't have to be super crafty or artistically inclined in order to make them! I created my first dream doll as a project for an Avalonian quest I was participating in. The assignment was to create something to honor or represent our connection to the Welsh goddess Arianrhod. My previous projects had typically been pieces of writing, music, or collages, mediums I was comfortable with. Based on my interactions with Arianrhod, I decided to stretch outside of my comfort zone for this particular project. While I believe I am a very creative person, I am not adept with a needle and thread. I ended up creating a simple dream doll with just a few materials and have found this dream doll to be very potent as an ally in dream magick. Feel free to tweak the following directions for making a dream doll as you see fit.

Making a Dream Doll
Materials Needed

+ Enough fabric to make your doll (I found an inexpensive bundle of square swatches of fabrics at a local craft store). The color and design of the fabric is completely up to you but should be something you associate with dreams and a dream-aligned ally or deity. Because Arianrhod is associated with the night sky, I used fabrics that were various shades of blues and silvers.
+ Cotton balls (enough to fill the fabric)
+ Sleep- or dream-aligned oils, herbs, and crystals, depending on your purpose for the doll
+ A needle and thread

Optional

+ Yarn for hair
+ Buttons, shells, or beads for facial features and decoration
+ Any other symbols you wish to incorporate

Instructions:

1. Draw an outline of the doll on a piece of paper. You will use this to cut your fabric to fit the pattern, so be sure to include features such as arms and legs. Be sure to cut two pieces of fabric using the outline.

2. Taking your needle and thread, sew the two pieces of fabric together in the shape of the doll. I used dark blue thread to match the color theme of my doll, but any color will do. Be sure to leave an opening somewhere at the top. This is where you will put the cotton balls.

3. Apply any oils that you wish to incorporate directly onto the cotton balls. (For a list of dream-aligned oils, herbs, and crystals, see appendix C.)

4. Stuff the cotton balls into the opening in the doll. Be sure to stuff it completely full of cotton balls so that there are no loose or sagging spaces in the doll.

5. Add any herbs and crystals that you wish to incorporate. You can also add written messages or symbols drawn on paper.

6. Finish sewing up your doll. Add any additional items or symbols such as yarn for hair, beads or buttons for eyes, or symbols that you wish to incorporate. Arianrhod is associated with the silver wheel of the night sky. I was able to find an inexpensive silver wheel charm at a local craft store, so I sewed that onto the doll's chest. I also added sparkly blue yarn to the doll for hair.

7. Sit in a quiet space in front of your dream altar (if you have one) holding the doll in your hand. Visualize and verbalize the intention you have for this doll. You may even want to do a guided journey to a place you associate with dreaming or with the deity or ally you have fashioned this doll after to dedicate the doll.

8. Finally, put the doll on your dream altar (or a general altar) or in some other sacred space and let it charge for a few days with the intention you have given it. I find this to be most helpful to do during a waxing moon phase. You can also charge the doll outside under the moon.

Your doll can have a permanent place on your dream altar or be placed directly beside you or under your pillow when you are doing dream work. If you are trying to activate a particular dream, you can write what you wish to dream about in a piece of paper and attach it to the doll with a safety pin. I recommend re-charging the doll every moon cycle for optimum benefit.

If you don't wish to create a doll, you can create a simple dream pillow using the same instructions. A much easier option if you don't wish to sew is to make a dream sachet. The benefit of creating a dream sachet is that it incorporates items that one may already have in their household and does not require any sewing. It also can be easier to travel with and less conspicuous as compared to a dream doll.

Making a Dream Sachet
Materials Needed

+ Clean piece of fabric that can be tied together such as a hand-kerchief, piece of felt, cloth napkin, or washcloth.
+ Ribbon or string
+ Cotton balls

Optional

+ Oils, herbs, and crystals: Mugwort, lavender, rose, and chamomile are all good basic dream herbs. (See appendix C for a more comprehensive list of oils, herbs, and crystals)
+ Sigils, messages, and symbolic items or pictures

Instructions

1. Take your fabric and lay it out flat.
2. Add cotton balls in the middle (oil infused if you prefer) as well as any other herbs, symbols, messages, or items you wish to include.
3. Fold all the ends together and tie the fabric with ribbon or string to make

it secure and so that none of the ingredients are at risk of coming out.

4. Sit in a quiet space in front of your dream altar (if you have one) holding the sachet in your hand. Visualize and verbalize the intention you have for this sachet. Finally, put the sachet on your dream altar (or a general altar) or in some other sacred space and let it charge for a few days with the intention you have given it. Again, I have found a waxing moon phase to be most appropriate. You can also charge the sachet under the moon.

The Use of Water in Dream Magick

As with any type of magick, doing some sort of ritual to bring you out of your mundane world and into a spiritual mindset is an important, foundational part of successful dream work. One great way to get into this mindset is a ritual bath. Water is known for being healing and purifying and is also associated in many cultures with accessing other realms. Prior to more modern inventions like cars and airplanes, journeys to other lands required crossing an ocean. Islands, which are typically thought of as liminal places, are accessible primarily by water.

In Celtic mythology, water plays a critical role in accessing liminal realms. In Irish mythology in particular, we find the concept of the *immram*: a journey across the sea and beyond the ninth wave to the Otherworld. In Greek tradition, bodies of water play a key role in crossing into the Underworld. The river known as Styx was established as a boundary to the Underworld that could only be crossed by paying the ferryman, Charon, with a special coin called an obol. For this reason, it was traditional to place a coin in or on the mouth of the deceased during funeral rites. While the world of dreams is technically not the same as the Underworld, there are many close associations between the two.

A ritual bath helps not only to cleanse us of our mundane thoughts and the energy we have accumulated during the day, it can also hearken back to our time in the womb. Parallels exist between the birthing process and our journey into the world of dreams: both the womb and the state of sleep can be places of comfort and darkness preparing us to be "born" into another world, and the womb is the gateway or starting point for travel into our human existence just as falling asleep leads us into the subconscious realm of dreams. Taking a ritual bath is a simple way to find a place of relaxation and calm as we prepare to transition into a state of sleep.

Ritual Bath for Dream Work
Instructions:

1. Fill a bathtub with water in the temperature range of warm to hot. The exact temperature is somewhat up to personal preference, but it should be warm enough that you will not get chilled if you are in the bath for a while nor so hot that it distracts you or causes you to want to end your bath prematurely.

2. Set the stage for your ritual bath by making sure as much as possible that you will not be disrupted. You may also want to add some additional elements such as candles and soft music. I personally like to turn off the lights and use regular or flameless candles surrounding the tub and soft, relaxing music at a very low volume.

3. Infuse your bath with herbs, oils, and flowers associated with your intent. As an example, I often use roses and lavender if my main goal is relaxation and herbs such as

mugwort and blue lotus if I am attempting prophetic or lucid dreaming. You can either place the herbs and oils directly in the bath or tie them in a small piece of cheese-cloth and place that on the faucet as the water is running or in the bath itself. As you lie in the bath, close your eyes and imagine that you are resting in a safe but liminal space. You could imagine you are in a womb or envision your bathtub as a cauldron. Immerse yourself in the feeling of being between two worlds as the water holds you and keeps you in a liminal space. Allow yourself some time to use as many senses as possible to experience your ritual bath: listen to the sound of the water moving around you, bring attention to the feeling of the water lapping against your skin. You may also want to do some deep, slow breathing to clear your mind and focus on the present moment.

4. When you feel sufficiently relaxed and open to the work ahead, think about your intent for your dreaming. If you are just starting out, you might simply focus on being in a peaceful, receptive state where you may fall asleep easily and be open to where your dreams may take you. You can even softly state, sing, or chant your intent.

5. If you are undertaking some advanced dream work such as lucid or prophetic dreaming, you can try doing carro-mancy, otherwise known as candle wax divination. Simply pour the hot wax from a candle into the water and note what images are made as the water hardens the wax. I have found this to be beneficial in providing symbols that I can look for or understand better in my dreams.

6. When you are ready, exit your bath and dry off before moving onto other pre-dream work activities or actually

heading to bed. Be sure to extinguish any burning candles. Doing these things in silence can greatly add to the transition to sleep.

7. Optionally, following your bath, you may want to undertake other pre-dream work activities referenced in this chapter.

USING SOUND

Sound can be a helpful tool in preparing to enter the dream world. Playing recordings of singing bowl music or shamanic drumming can be a great way to both relax into sleep and help our minds to become more receptive. Bells can also be beneficial as a way to condition our minds to prepare for dream magick. I will often ring a bell three times prior to going to sleep when I am doing dream magick as it signals to my brain that it is time to shift to a state that is more amenable to intentional dreaming. Over time, my mind has come to associate the bell with my intent so strongly that it often only takes one ring for my mind to begin to relax.

Chanting prior to going to sleep is another great way to set your intent. Well-known pagan chants such as "Spin, Spun, Spinning/ Weave, Woven, Weaving" can be used or you can use one of the chants below. You can also write your own chants. Due to the power of triads in Celtic and other traditions, I typically chant things in threes.

Chant for Restful Sleep

Lord/Lady of the Night
As the sunlight fades away
Help me to calm my mind and rest my body
So that I may sleep well and be ready for the day

Chant for Dream Weaving and Recall

Tonight I spin
Tonight I weave
The mosaic of my dreams
So I may dream of _____ this eve

Tonight the intent I have planted
For my dreams shall take root and flower
The picture clear
And remembrance true
Upon my waking hour

Chant for Inviting Your
Dream Ally Into Your Dreams

(Insert dream ally's name here), ally mine
I ask for your presence as I cross the line
From the waking world to the realm of dreams
Where often nothing is as it seems
Please guide me and protect me as I undertake this quest
So that my journey may be blessed

DREAM CONTROL

As part of my training in the early years of discovering Paganism and witchcraft, I learned a meditation technique designed to help me enter into my own magickal space in the astral realm. The original meditation technique never quite worked for me, but I was able to adapt the technique so that it would make more sense to me and therefore be more useful. The space I would travel to was mine and mine alone and was designed for me to be able to hone my craft and explore my abilities. Once I got beyond getting hung up on how to decorate my personal abode, I found this personal temple to be both a safe and comforting place.

The more I worked with and in this astral temple of mine, the more it would evolve and I would discover or invent features based on my needs and evolution of my craft. One of the most important tools that now exists in this realm is what I call the control panel. Hidden behind a picture on a wall is a panel that represents a variety of both magickal and mundane abilities. My control panel often includes things like empathy and intuition as well as states of being such as focus and relaxation. In my early exploration of this panel, I found that just as we have the ability to control the volume on a television, I could control the "volume" of each of the categories on the panel.

If I need to rely on my intuition more than usual, I would visit my control panel and turn the volume up on my intuition. If, as an empath, I found that I was taking on too much of other people's emotions, I could turn the volume down on my empathic abilities. As I progressed in my dream work, I found that I could incorporate abilities and perspectives related to dreaming as well. The dream work categories on my control panel include but are not limited to lucid dreaming, dream walking, dream recall, and intuitive dreaming. I have generally turned the volume up on these categories depending on the type of work I am doing and then turned them back to a neutral, midpoint position when not actively doing dream work.

After teaching a workshop on dream magick last year, an attendee came up to me and asked what she could do to actually *reduce* the quantity and vividness of her dreams. She explained that there were some nights where her dreams were so active and lifelike that it impaired her ability to get a restful night's sleep. This question made me realize that there can also be great benefit in using the control panel to turn the volume down on certain dream aspects, which can also be a great way to assist those who tend to have nightmares.

Here is a guided meditation designed to lead you to your own astral temple and, more specifically, your control panel.

For the control panel exercise to be effective, you will need to do it on a regular basis, especially in the early stages of your dream work. The more you work with your control panel, the more "real" it becomes to both the conscious and subconscious minds. In addition, I highly encourage you to keep a written journal that outlines the different categories you have worked with and what your results were. For maximum benefit, I recommend incorporating additional information into each entry such as moon phase, what time you went to bed, and any other dream work related activities you did prior to going to sleep. This can help you to pinpoint any factors that either enhanced or detracted from your control panel activities. The meditation below is most effective when done directly prior to going to sleep.

Control Panel Meditation

Sit or lie in a comfortable position in a space where you are not likely to be interrupted. Start by taking several deep, slow breaths in and out. When you feel that you are sufficiently relaxed, visualize a door in front of you. This can be any type of door-even a portal. When you are ready, you step through the doorway and find yourself walking down a pathway through a garden. As you approach the end of the pathway, you find yourself in front of a house. This house can be any kind of house. It may be the type of house you have always envisioned having or it may be something that surprises you. Regardless of whether the house is a grand castle or a cottage by the sea, the energy the house emits envelops you and you know that you are welcome in this place—it is yours and yours alone.

You reach into your pocket and pull out a key. This could be anything from an antique skeleton key to an object such as a crystal that fits neatly into the keyhole of the door. It might even be a sigil that you draw on the door of the house. Take a moment to study your key and then place your key into the lock. You hear or sense the lock giving way and step into your own private abode.

Take a moment to look around and explore. Both the inside of this building and the outside land it is sitting on seem to be built specifically to fit your preferences. The building and the land you are on feels safe, and the energy is uniquely yours. It is the energy you feel when you are at your best and when you are feeling happy, safe, and serene. The interior and exterior of this place may change over time but will always be designed to fit you perfectly and meet your needs in any given moment. When you have finished exploring your space, you turn your attention to a wall in your abode.

The wall is filled with a picture that has great meaning for you and that makes you feel secure, confident, and inspired. You approach the picture and find that as you reach out to touch it, it smoothly slides away to reveal a large control panel with categories and buttons that allow you to increase or decrease the intensity of each category. Take a moment to explore each of these categories. You may even want to experiment with some of the buttons to see how increasing or decreasing their intensity makes you feel. If you have come with a specific intent for your dream work, take a moment to increase or decrease the ability that most aligns with your intent. You may wish to state your intent as you use the control panel.

When you are ready, you touch the edge of the picture so that it slides back over the control panel. You walk out through the door and lock it before heading back up the path and back into your mundane reality. When you reach the doorway that you encountered at the start of this meditation, you walk back through and take several deep breaths to return to this reality. If needed, you may touch your hands and feet to the floor for additional grounding.

Please note that it is always a good idea to go back to your control panel the next day to reset any category you manipulated back to the midpoint. In my personal experience, not doing so can lead to overextending myself, which can result in feelings of burnout and fatigue.

Rose Visualization

If you do not have the time or energy to complete the control panel meditation above but still have dream work that you wish to undertake, you can use this simple visualization to access the abilities you wish to incorporate in your dream work. As with the control panel, this works best if you do it right before you head to bed. After taking a few moments to breathe deeply and settle into a receptive state of mind, imagine a tightly closed rose bud in your mind. Either state in your mind what it is you wish to accomplish (i.e., lucid dreaming, dream manifestation, etc.) or draw a sigil over the rose bud that represents the ability you wish to heighten or invoke. As you do so, imagine the rose bud beginning to unfurl and blossom until it reflects the level of intensity you are aiming for.

For example, if you are trying to maximize an ability, you would visualize the rose unfurling until it is fully in bloom. (I don't recommend doing this unless you have been doing dream work for quite some time. Starting at a lower level and working your way up over time will allow for better control of your dreamwork.) You can control the extent to which the rose blossoms based on the level of intensity you are aiming for. If you are just starting out with dream work, I suggest increasing the level of intensity a little at a time until you find the level of blossom that works best for you. Again, it is best to go back the next day and visualize the blossom reverting back to the tight rosebud as a reset to normal so that you don't exhaust your abilities or yourself.

As you begin to find success with the activities mentioned in this chapter, you will want to incorporate the information and techniques in the next chapter to remember and better understand the fruits of your labors.

Chapter 4
DREAM RECALL AND INTERPRETATION

If our conscious minds dominate during our waking hours, then it is fair to say that our subconscious mind takes control once we are sleeping. Our subconscious holds the shadows of our thoughts and feelings to the point that most of us go through our lives without ever truly being aware that the seeds of our actions often germinate in the dark yet fertile soil of this relatively hidden aspect of our minds. The analogy that makes the most sense to me is operating a vehicle tailored for a student driver: these vehicles typically have modifications so that both student driver and teacher can control the car. If the student driver needs help or in emergencies, the teacher can take control to avoid accidents.

In this analogy, the student driver—our conscious mind—thinks it is in full control of the vehicle without realizing that there is another entity—our subconscious mind—that is often able to take control of the vehicle without the former's knowledge. Many physicians and philosophers throughout history believed that the root of any problems or health issues we may have lie in our subconscious. The famous Greek physician Galen (129–216 CE) believed that illnesses were caused by "disharmonies of the soul."[43] It could also be said that our subconscious is responsible for patterns of choices and behaviors that do not serve us well throughout our lives.

The subconscious holds both the seed of some of our greatest challenges and behaviors that don't serve us. Yet, it also holds the treasure and the wisdom to help us break out of these patterns and realize our full potential. Although it sounds contradictory, modern science and psychology provides some explanation for why the subconscious can serve as both protagonist and antagonist in our lives. According to Richard Shwartz, developer of the Internal Family Systems Therapy, many of the behavior patterns we repeat that do not serve us started out as a way to protect us from or deal with trauma that occurred earlier in our lives. Schwartz asserts that all parts of our internal system or psyche—even those that are destructive—were formed "…in an attempt to protect the self system, no matter how much they now seem to threaten it."[44]

For the most part, we all tend to develop survival and coping mechanisms based on past hurts big or small. Unfortunately, the survival and coping mechanisms that may have once helped us often

43   Tick, *Dream Healing*, 132.
44   Bessel Van Der Kolk, *The Body Keeps the Score: Brain, Mind, and Body in the Healing of Trauma* (New York: Penguin Books, 2014), 285.

end up hurting us and stifling our potential as we grow older. If we want to get to the heart of what is hurting us or holding us back *and* access the power of our potential, we must learn the language of the soul and the subconscious. For this reason, dream recall and interpretation is vital. As author Nimue Brown points out, "paying attention to dreams is a way of reclaiming the wild, emotional, irrational, and often wiser self displaced by the pressures of modern living."[45]

Successful dream recall has been linked to improvements in both physical and mental health disorders. German researcher Michael Schredl conducted a study of individuals who participated in inpatient rehabilitation programs for addiction to alcohol. Schredl found that patients who had high dream recall of dreams about drinking shortly after undergoing rehabilitation were more likely to remain sober a year after ending the program.[46]

Despite the potential wealth of wisdom hidden inside of us, most of us don't realize the treasure that we possess let alone know how to access it. Many people tell me that they don't dream when the reality is that we all have, on average, at least six dreams each night.[47] Studies have shown that the average person only remembers their dreams once or twice a week. This means that anywhere from 95 to 99 percent of our dreams are forgotten.[48] This fact is not surprising given that most of us live in a society that does not value or pay attention to dreams.

The good news is that anyone can learn to improve their dream recall. It may take time as we peel away our disregard for our dreams in order to recondition our minds to see them as possessing valuable

---

45 Nimue Brown, *Pagan Dreaming: The Magic of Altered Consciousness* (Winchester, UK: Moon Books, 2015), 10.

46 Rock, *The Mind At Night*, 107.

47 LaBerge, *Lucid Dreaming*, 18.

48 LaBerge, *Lucid Dreaming*, 13.

information, but with patience and dedication it is possible. I have found that treating dream work in general as experimental play garners much faster and more reliable results than approaching dream work as a project that we must tackle and accomplish in a short period of time. Our often inherent tendency to strive for perfectionism can hinder our results. As with learning most new skills, we must give ourselves time and space to explore possibilities without having an immediate expectation of mastery.

IMPROVING DREAM RECALL

Astonishingly, two large factors in our ability to improve our dream recall are simply establishing intent and possessing a positive attitude. As Andrea Rock points out, simply having an interest in our dreams and a desire to remember them has been proven to have a strong correlation with increased dream recall. In my own experience, I have found that when I focus on and pay attention to my dreams, they become more vivid and easier to remember. This also seems to result in an increase in the number of dreams I have on any given night, which is something that Sigmund Freud hypothesized in the early 1900s.

There are other attributes that studies have shown to be associated with effective dream recall. For one thing, those who have high dream recall seem to have a stronger ability to produce visual imagery in their own minds during their waking hours. People who have a better than average ability to remember events from their childhood, daydream on a regular basis, and have an interest in visual arts also tend to have higher than average dream recall. In fact, individuals who have a creative mindset and an ability to think abstractly and theoretically tend to have a higher aptitude for dream work.

These factors have been validated via studies done by James Pagel, director of the Rocky Mountain Sleep Disorders Center.

Pagel's studies found that individuals who had a strong creative mindset had a dream recall that was almost twice that of the general population as well as having significantly more dreams that positively impacted their creativity in their daily lives.[49] There may be a biological reason for this. Andrea Rock writes that at least one dream scientist speculates that people who are drawn to abstract topics such as the arts and theoretical science tend to have brains wired to make connections that go beyond logic and analytical reasoning.[50] Fortunately, we all have the ability to improve and expand our creativity. One can find many activities and exercises for doing so online or via books.

There are other factors that affect our dream recall as well. Eating a healthy diet and getting sufficient sunlight exposure can strengthen serotonin levels, which in turn can make dream recall less difficult. Our dream periods become longer the more we sleep. The more dreams we have, the better the odds of remembering at least some of them. The actions we take upon waking can also have an impact on our ability to remember our dreams. Dream experts have asserted that we forget more than 50 percent of our dreams within five minutes of waking and 90 percent within ten minutes of waking.[51]

The time and way in which we wake up can influence both the types of dreams we have as well as our ability to remember them. Dreams that occur in the morning appear to be more vibrant than those occurring earlier in our sleep cycle. This is particularly true if we sleep past the time when we would normally awaken. Our body's internal clock seems to know when we are approaching our normal waking time, and our brain will begin to shift into a more active

---

49   Rock, *The Mind at Night*, 146.
50   Rock, *The Mind at Night*, 146.
51   Dylan Tuccillo, Jared Zeizel, and Thomas Peisel, *A Field Guide to Lucid Dreaming* (New York: Workman Publishing, 2013), 72.

mode. When we sleep later than we normally would, our internal clock shifts into this mode while we are still sleeping, resulting in dreams that are longer and more vivid and detailed than usual.

If we are to achieve maximum dream recall results, we must be mindful of the actions we take when we first wake up. It's not uncommon for many of us to play a game of tag with the snooze button on our alarm clock or—in more admirable cases—jump out of bed and immediately begin going about the day. However, both of these routines actually impede our ability to remember our dreams. Psychologist Hermann Rorschach, inventor of the famous inkblot test, observed in his dream studies that "quick motor movements" upon waking interfere with the ability to remember our dreams.

My own experiences as well as advice given by dream research professionals illustrate that dream recall attempts are best served by lying still when we first awaken and simply noting whatever we remember. You may not remember entire dreams at first, but remembering even fragments of dreams or images can help in eventually piecing together the narratives that played out in your mind while you were asleep. Slowly switching sleeping positions can also sometimes jog the memory. If you have some flexibility in your sleep schedule, you can try setting an alarm for an early morning hour (e.g., two or three o'clock) so that you can awaken for a short period to try remembering your dreams prior to falling back asleep. This may sound like odd advice, but research has shown that sleep interruption can actually help with dream recall.

The following guided meditation is another tool for improving dream recall. I suggest using this meditation on a regular basis prior to falling asleep. The more frequently you use it, the more your subconscious mind seems to associate it with finding your way back to your dreams. The meditation's imagery of the silver yarn has been particularly powerful for me; I often keep a piece of silver yarn by my bedside or on my dream altar as a symbolic key for activating dream recall as I lie still upon opening my eyes in the morning.

The Welsh goddess Arianrhod has been a supportive dream ally for me. Her alignment with the night sky and the silver wheel make her a natural ally in this work. Arianrhod's silver wheel is associated with the act of spinning and weaving yarn. In a similar fashion, we can view Arianrhod as weaving our dreams. This aligns with her role as an initiator in *The Mabinogion*, wherein the taboos she places upon her son, Llew, inspire him to take the actions necessary to become a man. The symbol of the silver yarn in this meditation relates to Arianrhod's talent in spinning and weaving with her silver wheel. *Caer Sidi* is the Welsh term for the fortress or castle where Arianrhod resides. Welsh mythology locates Caer Sidi in the Otherworld, but given Arianrhod's association with the Corona Borealis, she is sometimes also believed to reside in the starry sky. While both sites are liminal, the latter location of her residence fits well with this meditation's intention.

Guided Meditation: Journey to Caer Sidi

Pay attention to your breathing. When you are ready, imagine a door in front of you. Fix in your mind your intent to visit Arianrhod to request her assistance in your dream work. When you see the door in front of you and have this intent in your mind, walk through the door.

It is nighttime, and you find yourself at the edge of the ocean's shore. You can feel the damp air on your skin and you jump a bit as the frigid ocean water nips at your toes. In front of you is a narrow path that appears to take you to an island in the ocean. The tides are low, and the path is illuminated only by the heavy full moon overhead and what appear to be thousands of stars sparkling in the sky.

You take a deep breath, and begin making your way down the cold, rocky path. Although it takes some time, amazingly the tides seem to hold, and you have no problem finding your way. You notice that while you can make out the silhouette of the island, you can see nothing but mist, even as each step takes you closer to your destination. When you finally set foot onto the island, the mists separate and you see a silver and gold castle with spires rising high above the tallest of trees that surround it. You think to yourself that you need a moment before approaching the castle, and you turn back to the ocean. Kneeling on the shore at the edge of the island, you cup your hands to gather some of the ocean water. You notice the reflection of the starry night sky above rippling in the calm sea. Bracing yourself, you splash the water on your face and are stunned when you open your eyes again to see that the night sky is no longer reflected in the ocean; rather, the ocean has become the night sky.

You back away in astonishment and turn to find a woman standing before you. She is tall and stands erect, and she carries a spear in one hand. She possesses an unusual yet ethereal beauty and carries herself as a queen. You know at once that you have come face to face with Arianrhod. She beckons for you to follow her and you find yourself in a clearing.

"I am Arianrhod, goddess of the stars, time, and the tides. You have journeyed to my realm here at Caer Sidi. What is it you seek?"

You express your deep respect for Arianrhod and tell her of your desire to work with her in the realm of your dreams. Arianrhod is silent for a moment and then nods. You understand that she is willing to assist you, and you feel compelled to provide her with an offering. You offer her a gift in thanks for her help. She in turn gives you a symbol that will act as a key to help you return to this realm in the future. Take a moment to look closely at the symbol she has given you.

Arianrhod asks if you have a specific objective for this evening's dreams. You share with her your intent, and she directs you to stand facing two large, silvery birch trees. Arianrhod produces a beautiful, luminous silver thread. She motions for you to hold out your wrist, and you watch as she attaches the silvery thread around your wrist as though it were a bracelet. The thread is so lightweight that you don't feel anything other than a slight, pleasant buzz of energy. She sets the remainder of the attached thread into a crevice at the base of one of the trees. "When you wear this thread, it will help to record where you have traveled and what you have seen," she explains.

You turn back to the space between the two birch trees and notice that the space has been filled by glowing gold and silver threads of energy. From where you are standing, the energy feels warm, pleasant, relaxing and safe.

Arianrhod speaks again. "When you are ready to begin your dream work each evening, enter into a meditative state and simply use the symbol I have given you to make the dream portal appear before you. As you do so, the silver thread will appear on your arm. When you awake, simply use the thread to bring yourself back to the entrance by the birch trees and remove the silver thread from your wrist and place it in the crevice at the base of the tree. I will be here to assist you and answer your questions when the timing is right. You may then return on the path from which you came to Caer Sidi and walk back through the portal to return to your conscious, mundane reality."

You thank Arianrhod once again for her assistance. If you are ready to enter the dream realm, you follow her instructions into the portal. When you wish to return to the conscious *realm, simply walk back on the path that led you to Caer Sidi and through the portal near the forest. Pay attention once again to your breathing. When you are ready, open your eyes and record your experiences and dreams.*

Dream Journals

When people ask me for advice on how to remember their dreams, I often recommend keeping a dream journal. It is not uncommon for their response to include eyes that glaze over or a look that seems to say, "Really? Is that the best you can come up with?" It may not be the most glamorous or fun advice, but there is a reason that so many dream researchers throughout history have suggested keeping dream journals—because it works.

Even some of the most cynical people I have encountered have come back to me later to reluctantly admit that dream journaling significantly increased their recall. A coworker once told me that while her husband was in training as a Special Forces Green Beret officer, he and his fellow soldiers were instructed to keep a dream journal for a month. Despite thinking that a dream journal was some ridiculous New Age exercise that was ludicrous and beneath him, he did as instructed. After a month, he got rid of his journal and refused to ever do the exercise again not because it was as worthless as he believed it would be but because he began to remember his dreams more and recognized patterns and even prophetic dreams and it spooked him.

There are many benefits to keeping a dream journal, the most basic of which is that it helps to improve our dream recall. When you keep a record of your dreams, you begin to notice commonalities and patterns. You might find that certain actions, symbols, or locations appear in multiple dreams. Detecting patterns can help you recognize when you are in a dream, which can lead to dream lucidity. Keeping a journal also helps you sort out ordinary dreams from ones that may be unique and possibly meaningful. As Corinne Boyer points out, our unique dreams may "…have the potential to answer the questions of the seeker, by way of revelation with symbols, archetypes, motifs and patterns that is in the language only the dreamer can understand."[52]

For maximum effectiveness, keep your dream journal next to your bed so that you can easily record any fragments of dreams that you remember when you wake up each morning or if you happen to remember a dream in the middle of the night. As noted previously, minimal physical action upon waking can help jog the memory to recall dreams. Having a journal at the bedside minimizes movements you must make in order to capture your dreams. I recommend treating your dream journal like a travel diary. After all, you are traveling to another realm each time you sleep!

Describe each dream or fragment of dream as though you were an explorer entering a new land for the first time. What did you see? What were people doing? Was anything out of the ordinary occurring? The more details in your dream journal, the better. Details may include but are not limited to the following:

+ Dream title. It helps to give every dream a title of some sort, as though each dream were a unique story or adventure. Having a title for each dream can help you to more easily find them in your journal and may help you better recall your dreams as time goes by.
+ Date of the dream and time (if you know the time).
+ Lunar and astrological phases.

---

52 Boyer, *Dream Divination Plants*, 51.

+ Anything significant that you ate or did prior to going to sleep. (If you participated in one or more of the pre-dream work activities from chapter 3, note this as well.)

+ Write keywords associated with your dream. For example, if I had a dream that I got a new job, I might use keywords such as "job," "career," and "promotion."

+ Other participants. What other persons, animals, or other creatures appeared in your dream and what purpose did they serve? What were the interactions like? Sometimes interactions with other participants call attention to our relationship with these individuals in our waking lives, whereas other times the people in our dreams can act as representations of ourselves.

+ Sensory data. Use all of your senses when detailing your dreams. What did you see? Hear? Did you taste or smell anything in your dreams? While most dreams are visual, studies conducted in the 1890s found that more than half of dreams also contained auditory occurrences and roughly 15 percent included other senses such as touch, taste, and smell, though the last two are pretty rare.[53]

+ What did you feel both physically and emotionally? The latter is very important as oftentimes we wake up without a distinct memory of our dreams but with a strong emotional response. I have had dreams that have provoked a great sadness or fear upon waking even though the details of the dream eluded me. Sometimes simply recording the emotions we awaken with can help us remember the tone or theme of the dream later on.

---

53   Rock, *The Mind at Night*, 11.

+ Note any patterns. For example, I often dream of airports and flying on airplanes in my dreams. If you notice over time that certain patterns, images, or themes recur throughout your nocturnal travels, you will know to pay close attention as these patterns or themes often represent a deeply rooted message from your subconscious.

+ Document any unusual or enhanced dream occurrences. If you recall any notable occurrences such as dream lucidity, dream walking, intuitive dreams, and contact with the deceased, be sure to record this in your dream journal.

It is important to value and record every dream even if it seems inconsequential or absurd. While some dreams are difficult to describe as they defy time, space, or other parameters of our mundane reality, it is important to create entries for these dreams also even if all you can say about the dream is that it was complex or impossible based on our standards of waking reality. There are some commonalities that have been found as it relates to the types of dreams we have and this may help you with dream recall also. For example, what we do in our waking life can greatly influence the content of the dreams so that the things we focus on most during the day are more likely to show up in our dreams at night.

Dreams that occur earlier in the night are more likely to reflect what is occurring in our lives in the present whereas later dreams tend to include more of our past memories.[54] It is not uncommon for our dreams to also act as a catalyst for helping us pay attention to and process emotions, which may be why many people report having dreams in which they feel a high level of anxiety. Common anxiety dreams include:

---

54   Rock, *The Mind at Night*, 10.

- Taking a test you didn't study for
- Showing up to school or a meeting naked
- Being chased by someone or something
- An inability to move normally or to control your actions
- Public humiliation
- Having to use the bathroom in a public setting or in a room where the bathroom door won't shut
- Feelings of being lost and having a sense that something bad is about to happen

The longer you keep a dream journal, the more you will be able to not only better remember your dreams but also better understand what your dreams are trying to tell you. I have met many people who declined to keep a dream journal because writing was an arduous task for them or because they felt they didn't have time to write everything down. While writing can be the most detailed and common way of tracking dreams, it is certainly not the only method. If time is an issue or you are concerned that the act of writing will interfere with your recall, you can use a voice recorder (most smartphones tend to have one) to document your dreams.

Those who are more visually inclined may choose to draw a picture of their dreams. You could create a visual representation of actual scenes from your dreams or you can simply draw dream symbols that stuck out to you. You can even note specific songs or create a playlist of songs that you feel best describe your dreams. The most important thing is choosing a medium that you find easy to commit to on a daily basis and that is effective in documenting all of the dream details you can recall. I strongly suggest waiting at least two weeks before looking at the entries in your dream journal as I find that identifying dream patterns and attempting dream interpretation becomes easier the more entries you have to work with.

METHODS OF DREAM INTERPRETATION

While recording dreams is critical, to truly get the most out of our nighttime travels we must try to understand what it is our dreams—and therefore our subconscious—are trying to tell us. Sigmund Freud believed that interpreting our dreams was the "…'royal road' to understanding the unconscious activities of the mind."[55] Interpretation can be challenging because the subconscious mind often doesn't communicate in the direct manner of the conscious mind, preferring instead to use symbols to communicate.

There tends to be similar dream content across cultures, locations, and backgrounds, which may be how dream dictionaries came into being, though they are thought to have originated with the ancient Greeks. Their dictionaries were built on the premise that all dreams consist of symbols and that symbols have universal meanings. It is true that looking at common symbols and archetypes across cultures can be a helpful approach when it comes to dream analysis. However, dream dictionaries typically don't work for most people, at least not on a deep level. For one thing, history shows us that many symbols have meanings that differ by culture. Owls are said to represent wisdom in many cultures, but an exploration of feng shui shows that Chinese philosophy also associates the owl with prosperity, whereas the myths of the Navajo culture indicate that the owl was sometimes seen as a harbinger of bad news.[56]

Our subconscious holds the key to the truths hidden in the shadows of our psyche. Our dreams can often be a treasure map

---

55   Rock, *The Mind at Night*, 7.
56   Harold Carey Jr., "Owl and Woodpecker—A Navajo Tale," Navajo People website, January 9, 2015, https://navajopeople.org/blog/owl-and-woodpecker-a-navajo-tale/.

leading us to the answers we seek if we can only read the map. If we truly want to understand what our subconscious is trying to tell us in our dreams, then we need to learn its language and that language is, for the most part, uniquely our own. What represents one thing to one person might symbolize something completely different to someone else.

During a workshop, I asked the attendees to write down what an apple symbolized for them. I then had attendees share their answers, and they were pretty diverse. For some, the apple represented health (as in "an apple a day keeps the doctor away"), whereas for others it represented the biblical Eden or the mythical island of Avalon where King Arthur is said to be buried. One woman associated apples with love because her son had once planted an apple tree for her as a gift. As the authors of *A Field Guide to Lucid Dreaming* assert, "… since our dreams are a tapestry woven from personal symbols, archetypes, and waking life details, it seems fair to say that the dream world is the actual Embodiment of our larger minds."[57]

While exploring general archetypes, myths, and symbols may at times provide guideposts and possibilities, I believe that truly the only person who can crack the code of their dreams is the dreamer.

Creating a Personal Dream Dictionary

Creating your own personal dream dictionary can be an extremely powerful tool in decoding your dreams. This dictionary is intended to be a living, evolving document that should be reviewed and revised from time to time. Just as our opinions, tastes, and mindsets can change as we get older, so too can the meanings we associate with specific symbols, images, or ideas. For this reason, I suggest reviewing your dream dictionary at least once a year.

---

57   Tuccillo, Zeizel, and Peisel, *Field Guide to Lucid Dreaming*, 25–26.

The best time to create a dream dictionary is early in your dream magick efforts. You can start by simply writing in a blank journal or notebook a number of common words, items, and symbols, leaving space underneath each entry for your interpretations. You may want to categorize these words and symbols either alphabetically or by frequency. As you look at each word, write down whatever immediately comes to mind for you, whether it's one meaning or image or multiple interpretations. Whatever you do, don't overthink it. Because we are dealing with our subconscious, typically the first thing or things that come to mind are the interpretations that resonate.

After you have begun your dream dictionary, if you notice over time that certain symbols or words appear often in your dreams, you may want to write down additional information such as what tarot card, element, or rune you associate this symbol with. This can be beneficial as you undertake activities later in this chapter designed to help you gain clarity about the deeper meaning of some of your repetitive dreams. Some common words or symbols to get your dream dictionary started are as follows:

+ Acts of nature (e.g., tornadoes, wildfires, earthquakes)
+ Amusement parks (and amusement park rides)
+ Apple
+ Appliances (e.g., washers, dryers, refrigerators, ovens)
+ Bed
+ Birds
+ Blanket
+ Bones
+ Books
+ Cat
+ Cauldron or chalice

- Classroom
- Feasts
- Food
- Forest
- Green (color)
- Hat
- Holidays
- Hospital
- House
- Masks
- Mountains
- Night sky
- Ocean
- Office
- Red (color)
- Rocking chair
- Sword
- Teeth
- Trees
- Vehicles (i.e., cars, boats, trains, airplanes—each will likely have a separate meaning)

Other Dream Interpretation Activities

Divination: Divination tools such as tarot or oracle cards, runes, and bones can provide a deeper exploration into the meaning of our dreams. I often use tarot and oracle cards when I am having a difficult time cracking the code of a particular dream. Sometimes I will pull cards from a traditional tarot deck of a suit I associate with the theme of my dream and then look for a card within that suit that resonates with me. Other times, I will go through my oracle and tarot decks looking for an image that somehow relates to the dream in question.

For example, one of my decks has a tarot card showing a mountain with a hidden entrance at its base. I might use this card to further explore a dream I had involving a secret cave. I will then get into a meditative state and envision myself entering the card as though it were a tangible landscape. Exploring the landscape and talking to figures in the card often leads me to answers that I might otherwise not have found. The same can be done with other divination tools such as runes; instead of visualizing an image, you might visualize entering a structure or door comprised of the rune.

If you are looking for simple yes/no answers about your dream, dowsing rods and pendulums can also be of help.

Dream sharing: Sometimes simply talking about our dreams with others can help us garner invaluable insights, both due to the process of talking about our dream out loud and having others provide fresh perspectives. One way of doing this is to establish a dream sharing circle where you and other like-minded individuals share one or more dreams that you wish to gain more clarity about. Each participant has the opportunity to share a dream and agrees to silently listen to others dreams while they are being described. Rather than sharing their own interpretation of the dream, participants may ask questions to help the dreamer peel away the layers of confusion surrounding the dream.

Automatic writing: Automatic writing has been extremely beneficial for me when I have hit a wall in my dream interpretation. Perhaps this is because automatic writing taps into the subconscious itself. When doing automatic writing, you can ask about a specific component of your dream or simply think about the dream and begin writing. You will want to do this activity in a quiet place with gentle meditative techniques as a precursor so that you are in a receptive state of mind. When you are ready, simply start writing without thinking about or looking at what words are being put on paper. If you are having trouble getting anything to come to mind, try writing with your non-dominant hand—it can sometimes help us connect with the intuitive and untapped aspects of our brain.

The more we can improve our dream recall and establish a dialogue with our dreaming self, the more effectively we can do other types of dream magick, including intuitive and lucid dreaming, which follow in subsequent chapters.

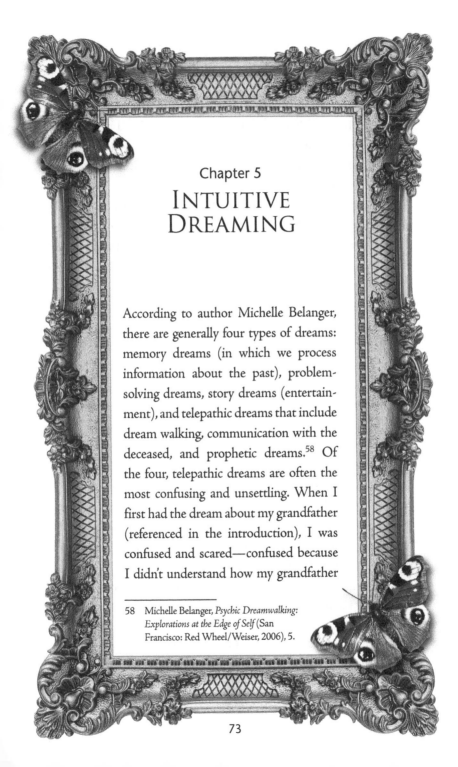

Chapter 5

INTUITIVE DREAMING

According to author Michelle Belanger, there are generally four types of dreams: memory dreams (in which we process information about the past), problem-solving dreams, story dreams (entertainment), and telepathic dreams that include dream walking, communication with the deceased, and prophetic dreams.[58] Of the four, telepathic dreams are often the most confusing and unsettling. When I first had the dream about my grandfather (referenced in the introduction), I was confused and scared—confused because I didn't understand how my grandfather

58   Michelle Belanger, *Psychic Dreamwalking: Explorations at the Edge of Self* (San Francisco: Red Wheel/Weiser, 2006), 5.

was able to communicate with me if he had died and I wasn't even sure if what I had dreamed was real, and scared to tell anyone about my dream because they might not believe me or they'd think something was wrong with me. Given that I already received more than my fair share of attention due to my rare medical condition, the last thing I wanted was to give anyone another reason to label me abnormal.

Like many other children with this type of experience, on some level I tried to shut down my intuition so that my dreams would go back to normal. On those occasions when telepathic dreams snuck through my defenses, I would stubbornly ignore them and keep them to myself. Despite my best efforts, I continued to have telepathic dreams from time to time but rarely shared them with anyone else. Finally, when I was in college I had a dream that an apartment complex had burned down but fortunately no one was badly hurt. I could see the apartments in great detail in my dream.

The next day as I was driving to my boyfriend's house, I happened to pass by what looked like an apartment building that had recently been partially destroyed in a fire. I gasped as I realized that the apartment building looked exactly like the one I had seen in my dreams! When I got to my boyfriend's apartment, I told him about the dream and we turned on the news. Sure enough, there was a report about a fire at an apartment building the previous night but the reporters reassured viewers that no one was severely injured. My boyfriend, who was a little more open to metaphysical occurrences than my previous boyfriends had been, looked me in the eye and told me that it was time for me to stop running from whatever psychic ability I had and to start learning more about it.

PROPHETIC DREAMS

One of the most confusing things about prophetic dreams is that it can be difficult to differentiate between what is a prognostic dream versus a dream that is simply the subconscious playing out memories or the day's events. The best way to determine which is which is keeping a detailed record of your dreams and noting any peculiarities or ways that some dreams feel different. When you find that some dreams have been validated as foretellings, you can go back through your journal and look for patterns that occur only or mostly with your dreams that are predictive or divinatory in nature. I have found that my prophetic dreams tend to be more vivid and detailed than ordinary dreams.

When we talk about divination in Pagan or metaphysical circles, the focus is mostly on phenomena such as tarot cards, scrying, having visions, or merely having a sense about something. Yet, dream divination is found across many cultures and is one of the oldest methods of prophecy. As Caitlin Matthews points out, "Dream is the portal of seership that we all share."[59] Even noted psychologists such as Freud and Jung recognized that in addition to shedding light on our subconscious, dreams could also be predictive.

The ruins of oracles found throughout Greece are a testament to the ancient Greeks' belief that dreams could predict the future. Perhaps the most famous example the Oracle of Delphi. Ancient Greeks believed that the Pythia of the Delphi could not only predict the future using dreams but also diagnose and treat illness.

The practice of dream prophecy and incubation is believed to originate from a tradition in Asia Minor as evidenced by the oracle sites at Mopsos in Cilicia and Telmessians in Caria.[60] Ancient Sumerian kings also seemed to believe in the power of dream incubation and prophecy as they were known to sleep at the top of their

---

59   Caitlin Matthews, *Celtic Visions: Seership, Omens and Dreams of the Otherworld* (London: Watkins Publishing, 2012), 37.

60   Walter Burkert, *Greek Religion: Archaic and Classical* (Cambridge, MA: Harvard University Press, 1987), 115.

temples in hopes of having a sacred dream that would reveal to them the answers they were seeking.[61] Ancient Chinese records from the Zhou dynasty also indicate that oneiromancy—divination by dreams—was an important and often-used method for predicting the future.

Divination via dreams is also prevalent in Celtic mythology and practices. Two divinatory practices in particular are well-attested in written records and stories from the Irish Druidic traditions. These are the Tarbh Feis and the Imbas Forosnai. The Ulster Cycle of Irish mythology contains a story entitled "*Togail Bruidne Dá Derga*," or "The Destruction of Da Derga's Hostel." In this tale, the Tarbh Feis or bull feast was held as part of a ritual to determine who would be king.

A white bull was said to be sacrificed and a broth made from its flesh. It was believed that eating the bull would help induce a deep sleep.[62] Once the feast had ended, a seer—most likely a Druid— would wrap himself in the skin of the bull.[63] Setting his intention to learn who should be the next king, he would then retire to a north-facing bed made out of rowan wood and steeped in ritual and magic while other Druids chanted over him. When the seer awoke, he would proclaim who he had seen in his dreams as that person was destined to be the next king. It was said that if the seer lied, he would die.[64] While "The Destruction of Da Derga's Hostel" specifically referenced the use of Tarbh Feis for determining who should be king, there is evidence to indicate that the Druids used this ritual to gain other types of knowledge such as to predict the outcome of a future battle.

---

61   Belanger, *Psychic Dreamwalking*, 26.
62   Morpheus Ravenna, *The Book of the Great Queen: The Many Faces of the Morrigan from Ancient Legends to Modern Devotions*, (Richmond, CA: Concrescent Press, 2015), 306.
63   Matthews, *Celtic Visions*, 334.
64   Lora O'Brien, "Irish Pagan Magic—The 'Tarbh Feis,'" Lora O'Brien—Irish Author & Guide website, July 24, 2018, https://loraobrien.ie/irish-pagan-magic-tarbh-feis/.

Imbas Forosnai was a different type of ritual, though it does have similarities to the Tarbh Feis. In Old Irish, *imbas* means "inspiration" and *forosnai* translates to "illuminate." It appears in the well-known Irish myth, "Táin Bó Cúilange" and was said to be used by the goddess Scathach and the well-known Irish figure Fionn mac Cumhaill.[65] In the Imbas Forosnai, the seer would chew on a piece of raw animal flesh, such as that of a sow, cat, or dog, and would then place the chewed flesh behind on a flagstone near the door of the room in which they were sequestered for the remainder of the ritual.

The seer would then chant incantations over the chewed flesh before finally retiring to sleep with the intent of having a prophetic dream. The ritual sleep could occur in a building designated for sacred rites or in tombs or cairns. Other Druids watched over the seer and guarded the ritual space to ensure it was not disturbed. While traditionally it has been said that the seer would accomplish the prophetic dream by the end of three days and three nights, other sources say that it could take as long as nine days and nights to receive a prophecy.[66]

In 2017, I was fortunate enough to take part in an adapted ritual that had strong similarities to the Imbas Forosnai and was astonished at what I experienced. A small group of fellow sisters and I visited Stony Littleton Long Barrow, a Neolithic chambered tomb constructed in roughly 3500 BCE. After taking some time to get into a meditative state of mind, we crouched down to enter the tomb and were instructed to lay down in one of the burial chambers within the tomb. This was rather difficult for me as I tend to

---

65   "Imbas Forosnai", Oxford Reference, last accessed August 2023, https://www
     .oxfordreference.com/display/10.1093/acref/9780198609674.001.0001/acref
     -9780198609674-e-2760.

66   Ravenna, *Book of the Great Queen*, 307.

be claustrophobic and, as you can imagine, the space was very small. The fact that it was also very dark certainly didn't help.

I persevered because I had received clear indications from one of the deities that I work most closely with that this ritual was important for my spiritual goals and growth. Despite my fear of spiders and other critters lurking in the dark, I curled up in a burial chamber off to the side of the tomb and tried to find a comfortable position laying down on the gravel beneath me. We started the ritual by chanting until our voices started to collectively fade away. Eyes closed, I tried to let go and clear my mind. Within a few minutes, I began to clearly see a landscape around me as though my eyes were open.

The images and answers that came to me during this ritual were powerful and emotional, and the same was true for my fellow participants. It was as though I had experienced a waking dream, and the information I received in the midst of this experience proved to be eerily accurate and helpful in the days and months to come. Oddly enough, when it was time to end the ritual, I was so comfortable that it was hard for me to leave the tomb.

While it may not be practical to re-create the Tarbh Feis and Imbas Forosnai in specific detail, my experience in Stony Littleton Long Barrow led me to adapt a ritual with similar elements that can be done in the privacy of your own home called the ritual of illumination. It can be done either right before going to sleep for the night or as part of a shorter duration of sleep.

The ritual is most effective if done in an area where you can be assured you won't be disrupted for the entirety of the experience. While the Tarbh Feis focuses on eating meat as a way to drift into a heavy sleep, I find that eating meat or a full meal before undertaking something like this actually interferes with the effectiveness of this ritual, but each person is unique; I encourage you to do what works best for you. This ritual does not include chewing on any animal flesh. However, if you are having difficulty concentrating or settling your mind during the ritual, you could try putting the tip of your thumb in your mouth so that it touches the roof of your mouth. I suggest closing your lips around the thumb. It may sound like an odd suggestion, but it actually hearkens back to the myth of the great seer Fionn mac Cumhaill, who was said to be able to gain wisdom and foretell the future simply by putting his thumb in his mouth.

Ritual of Illumination

1. Find a space where you won't be interrupted. Small spaces such as closets can work very well for this. If you tend to get claustrophobic or don't have access to a small space, an ordinary room will work just fine.

2. Cast a circle around your space and ward your space with your dream allies standing guard.

3. Focus on your intent for this ritual in your mind or state it out loud. If there are specific answers you are looking for, state that as well.

4. Lay down in a comfortable position with a weighted blanket or a variety of blankets on top of you. This helps to re-create the element of the Tarbh Feis ritual wherein the seer covers themselves in the bull hide. Personally, I find that having a weighted blanket (or multiple heavy blankets) on top of me helps me to settle and clear my mind and feel safe.

5. Either chant or play trance inducing music such as shamanic drumming. If you are playing music, set it up so that it automatically stops at a certain time, and even better if it can fade out. If you are chanting, be sure to stop at some point.

6. Prior to or as soon as the chanting or music stops, close your eyes. I highly recommend using a weighted eye pillow or sleep mask to ensure utter darkness, which is a critical element in this ritual.

7. As you focus on the answers you seek, let your body relax into the ground and pay attention to the images that come to your mind. (If you don't typically get visual information, you may also want to focus on any sounds you hear or feelings that come over you). Gently follow the information where it takes you without judgment. The analogy I like to use is thinking of yourself as a passenger in a car: you are not steering the vehicle, you are simply enjoying the scenery.

8. When you are ready, remove the sleep mask or eye pillow and open your eyes. You can either let yourself be guided into sleep and wake up as you normally would or, if you are aiming for a shorter ritual, set a timer to bring you back to the mundane world.

9. Release any circles you have cast and wards you have placed.

10. Be sure to document your experiences.

PLANT ALLIES

Plants can be powerful allies in dream work. There are many plants that can act as catalysts for dream magick and many myths and folklore beliefs that reference the connection between plants and dream magick. Corinne Boyer, author of *Dream Divination Plants in the Northern European Tradition*, refers to many folklore beliefs about the use of plants in prophetic dreaming including but not limited to the use of plants for general prophetic dreams such as grave grass

(England), blackberry thorns, apples under the pillow (Cornwall), ivy leaves (British Isles and Ireland), holly and ivy together, mistletoe (Ireland), oats (Russia), pine needles (Scotland), hazel trees, Western red cedar trees (west coast Native Americans), and elder tree branches.[67] In most cases, these plants or branches were placed under the dreamer's pillow or the dreamer would be instructed to sleep under the tree.

Some recipes required plants to be gathered and that the dreaming occur at a specific time. In several cases, numbers were significant such as the need to collect plants in threes or nines. One example of this is a Northumberland tradition that recommended gathering holly leaves in a three-cornered handkerchief on a Friday evening. Nine leaves were to be placed in the handkerchief, which was then to be tied in nine knots and left under the pillow to facilitate prophetic dreaming.[68]

Not surprisingly, many of these folkloric beliefs focused on using dreams to get answers about one's love life. Ingredients for these recipes included seeds such as linen, hemp, and dock as well as herbs such as marigold, wormwood, thyme, marjoram, and oregano.[69] The latter herbs were used to make a potion so that a young lady could dream of her future husband. A very specific recipe from *Dream Divination Plants in the Northern European Tradition* instructs a maiden to peel a red onion on December 21 and stick it with nine pins; eight to be place in a circle on the onion and the ninth in the middle.[70] The middle pin would represent the man the maiden wanted to marry. She would then speak an incantation of

---

67   Boyer, *Dream Divination Plants*, 25, 26, 35–37, 39.

68   Boyer, *Dream Divination Plants*, 34.

69   Boyer, *Dream Divination Plants*, 26.

70   Boyer, *Dream Divination Plants*, 36–37.

some sort and place the onion under her pillow with the hopes that her dreams would tell her if the young man would be hers.[71]

Perhaps one of the most well-known dream divination ingredients in ancient Greek history is the bay tree, which was believed by many to aid in prophecy during sleep. Bay leaves, otherwise known as bay laurel or sweet bay, were famously used by the Pythia at the Oracle of Delphi to induce divine inspiration that would in turn lead to prophetic messages. The following ritual uses bay leaves as a primary ingredient to invoke intuitive dreams. Sometimes it can be helpful to ask for general insight rather than asking a specific question; sometimes we don't know what we need to know. This ritual focuses on inducing a dream to help us understand what our subconscious feels is the most important information we can have at this time in our lives, but it can be adapted to ask about specific questions.

Bay Leaf Ritual
Materials Needed

- Paper and pen
- Felt marker
- Cauldron (or other heatproof container)
- Bay leaf
- Lighter or matches
- White candle
- Symbol for the Pythia (this could be anything that you associate with these women, such as a statue or visual image of a priestess, a bay tree branch, or a scrying bowl)
- A small baggie, handkerchief, or cloth bag

---

71   Boyer, *Dream Divination Plants*, 36–37.

Instructions

1. Start by casting a circle as you normally would. Facing the representation of the Pythia, ask for their help in your quest for intuitive answers once you fall asleep.

2. On the piece of paper, write your question. For general questions, I typically write things such as, "What is the most important thing I need to know at this point in my life," "What is holding me back and how can I overcome it," or "What action or actions should I be taking right now for greater happiness and to fulfill my potential?" Once you have written your question, place it in the cauldron.

3. Using the felt marker, draw a symbol or sigil on your bay leaf that you associate with intuition, clarity, or knowing. For example, I often use the symbol of a key, a flashlight (to see in the dark), or an eye. Your symbol should be easy to remember and have a strong correspondence with intuition and finding answers. Light the bay leaf from the candle's flame and place it in the cauldron so that it also ignites the paper placed inside.

4. Sit in silence as you watch the bay leaf and the paper burn. When the fire has gone out and the ashes are cool to the touch, place the ashes in your bag. Place the bag under your pillow prior to falling asleep. In the morning, be sure to record any images, clues or messages that appeared in your dreams. (Note: If you receive messages or symbols in your dreams but need more clarity as to their meaning, it can sometimes be helpful to scry with water, a crystal, or a mirror to get more clarity).

Drinking a special tea blend shortly before going to sleep (such as the one in the recipe that follows) can enhance your efforts in inducing prophetic dreams. Mugwort has long been known to aid in psychic abilities, especially as it relates to dreams. Mint leaves are said to be able to help dreams become more vivid and more likely to be remembered. Ancient Egyptians were reputed to use blue lotus flowers, a plant associated with the sun god, Ra that has psychoactive properties. Blue lotus is said to promote feelings of ease and euphoria and is also known for its tendency to promote vivid dreaming as well as lucid dreaming. Finally, rose petals help with relaxation and a gentle transition into the world of dreams.

I have found the effects of this tea to be subtle yet effective. I recommend starting with a very small dose and slowly working your way up until you find the dose that works best for you.

Intuitive Dream Tea Recipe

Note: Do NOT use this tea if you are pregnant or if you suspect you may have allergies to any of the ingredients. Also, mugwort and blue lotus should not be taken in large doses. Be sure that any herbs you use have not been treated with chemicals.

Ingredients

- One part dried mugwort leaves
- One part dried or fresh mint leaves
- One part dried blue lotus petals
- ½ part dried rose petals

Steep the tea for roughly five minutes in boiling water. Mugwort can be bitter, so you may want to add honey or sugar to make it more palatable.

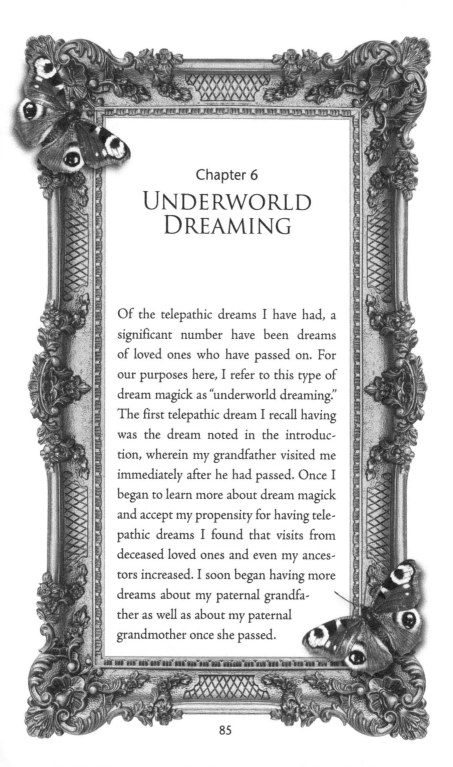

Chapter 6
UNDERWORLD DREAMING

Of the telepathic dreams I have had, a significant number have been dreams of loved ones who have passed on. For our purposes here, I refer to this type of dream magick as "underworld dreaming." The first telepathic dream I recall having was the dream noted in the introduction, wherein my grandfather visited me immediately after he had passed. Once I began to learn more about dream magick and accept my propensity for having telepathic dreams I found that visits from deceased loved ones and even my ancestors increased. I soon began having more dreams about my paternal grandfather as well as about my paternal grandmother once she passed.

My maternal grandmother became an ongoing presence in my dreams while my maternal grandfather was still alive. In fact, she was the one who let me know even before my grandfather had been formally diagnosed with cancer that he was sick and was not long for this world. At the time, my grandfather did not appear to me to be ill. My maternal grandfather and grandmother had a love story for the ages and appeared to be in some ways almost psychically connected while they were both still alive. My grandfather had shared with me after her death that he frequently had dreams of her that brought him comfort, and these dreams seemed very real.

These types of dreams didn't always occur directly after my loved one had passed; sometimes it took time, and other times the deceased would appear in my dreams shortly after their death but would not speak to me until several months later. This was the case when I unexpectedly lost my eighteen-year-old niece, Anam. We were very close, so I wasn't surprised when she showed up in my dreams the night following her passing. What did surprise and frustrate me was that while she was there, she would not speak to me.

I was disappointed about this both because we were very close and because we had conversations about her strong intuition, vivid dreams, and other extrasensory abilities when she was alive. Months later, after I had finally begun to process my grief, she began showing up in my dreams in a more engaging way. Sometimes she took the form of her childhood self and in others she was the age that she had been when she passed. Each time she shared a little more with me and comforted me by telling me that she was doing well and that someday I would understand more.

I have also had dreams of friends who have passed but in some cases could not or would not speak to me; rather, they would only smile and hug me. My dreams of the deceased are not limited to loved ones of the human variety. I have had many appearances of beloved pets in my dreams and continue to do so. In one case, a cat that I was particularly bonded with acted as a guide, bringing me together with another animal in need of a home.

Several months after my cat, Topaz, had passed, I had been thinking of getting another one but hadn't yet found one that seemed like the right fit. I had a dream in which Topaz led me into a room where I found an older female tortoiseshell cat waiting for me. The next day as I was looking through available pets on a Humane Society website, I found an older female cat that looked exactly like the cat I saw in my dream the night before.

This cat, Callie, was unlikely to be adopted because of her age. In addition, she had previously been in a home that was neglectful and I suspect she may have been subject to abuse at some point in her life. I adopted her, and while it took her some time to trust me, we eventually ended up forming a close bond. I would never have expected for a dream to lead me to a new four-legged friend, but I believe that the love Callie and I shared helped us both to heal.

COMMON TRAITS OF DREAM VISITATIONS

I have learned to put my expectations aside and be open to what I receive. Having done that, I find that visitations from those I have lost happen more frequently and are in many ways more meaningful. I have also learned that deceased loved ones don't always appear in dreams immediately following their death for what I believe are a few reasons. In some cases, it seems as though the deceased—human or animal—need some time to orient themselves to life after death before they can begin to reach out to those they left behind. If the deceased possessed feelings of shame or regret prior to their passing, they may be hesitant to reach out to their loved ones.

Sometimes the disconnect can be on our end. As discussed in previous chapters, certain substances such as alcohol, sleeping pills, or marijuana, can actually make it more difficult for us to be receptive to visitations from our loved ones, or it may be that these visitations occur but these substances make it difficult for us to remember our dreams the following morning. Our own fear of our telepathic dream abilities can create a blockage. Another possibility is that we are not truly ready to interact with our deceased loved ones. We may still be trying to come to terms with their death, or there may be some unresolved feelings about our relationship with the person.

My father passed away as I was writing this book, and I was disappointed that as of the one-month anniversary of his passing, he had not visited me in my dreams. However, I believe that this may have been because I had not fully processed my grief or feelings about his death and instead had been focused on helping my family with the aftermath of his passing. I did feel his presence around me, so I learned to be patient. In talking with my husband one night, I lamented that I would have liked to have had one more Christmas with my dad.

Shortly before finishing this book, I had a dream that my immediate and extended family members were in a house together with a huge, vibrantly lit Christmas tree and an almost ridiculous amount of food and presents. We were all laughing and enjoying ourselves when I noticed that it had begun to softly snow outside. It was as if we were having the picture-perfect holiday. At one point, I noticed my father by the Christmas tree. He looked younger, healthier, and happy. I approached him and thanked him for giving me this one last Christmas with him in my dreams. He smiled at me and said, "Thank *you*. I love you, baby doll." This visitation meant the world to me and further reinforced my faith in the ability for those who have crossed over to visit with us as we sleep.

One of the biggest challenges in this type of dream work is differentiating between a "normal" dream and a true visitation. This is another area in which recording your dreams and noting specific details can come in handy. In my personal experience, visitations from the deceased are often marked by a distinct difference in what is occurring in the background of the dream. There is usually something occurring in the background of these dreams but it is fuzzy, whereas the interaction between myself and the deceased is very vivid and clear. It is almost as though everything but the interaction between the two of us is simply there to serve as some sort of white noise or background against which a play is set.

In some cases, there is a noticeable deviation in interactions between the deceased and myself as compared to interactions between the deceased and others in the dream. For example, in my dreams with my niece, it is not uncommon for our conversations to be marked with a distinct sharpness or vibrancy; everything is crystal-clear. When she talks with others in the dream, the visual effects are softer and hazier, and it is hard to make out what's being said. The other unique quality I have noticed about my visitation dreams with Anam is that while it is clear in my interactions with Anam that we both know she is deceased, others in the dream do not. I recommend making notes about these kinds of details in your dream journal.

UNDERWORLD DREAMING THROUGHOUT HISTORY

There is plenty of evidence to indicate that our ancestors attempted to reach the world of the dead via their dreams. Corinne Boyer states that, "Dreaming has long been thought to be an entrance into the spirit world...."[72] There are many accounts across history and cultures of people either spontaneously dreamed of the dead or where people would sleep on or near the graves of the dead in order

---

72   Boyer, *Dream Divination Plants*, 15–16.

to access the wisdom of the deceased. These incidences occurred throughout ancient Gaul and Ireland where there was a belief that a dreamer could visit the liminal realm and bring back invaluable knowledge, be it predictions of the future or other meaningful information. Ancient Egyptian cultures worked with Anubis, god of the dead, for divination purposes. In fact, many deities who are psychopomps are also associated with dream magick.

Studies support the idea that underworld dreaming has been experienced in many cultures. According to researcher Kai Chang-Yu, "…seeing a person now dead as through alive was dreamed by 46 percent of American participants, 38.4 percent of Canadian participants, 51.4 percent of Chinese participants, 45 percent of German participants, and 57.4 percent of Japanese participants in the same studies conducted in different countries."[73]

Plant folklore of Northern Europe refers to the use of various plants as allies in seeking dream visitations from the dead. These plants include but are not limited to the roots of English daisy, thyme, rosemary, and wormwood.[74] Despite all the research and folklore that point to the existence of Underworld dreams, some may find it impossible or difficult to accept that it can actually occur. From a practical standpoint, however, dreams are the perfect vehicle for making contact with the deceased.

How Does Underworld Dreaming Work?

Unlike our waking world, the world of dreams offers limitless possibilities. Our dreams are not restricted by the parameters of our mundane world. Laws of space and time do not apply to dreams. Many

---

73   Calvin Kai-Ching Yu, "Imperial Dreams and Oneiromancy in Ancient China—We Share Similar Dream Motifs with Our Ancestors Living Two Millennia Ago" *Dreaming: Journal of the International Association for the Study of Dreams* 32, no. 4, (March 2022): 364.

74   Boyer, *Dream Divination Plants*, 27, 46.

people I talk to have had dreams that were difficult if not impossible to describe because they did not follow the logic of our waking existence. I have had dreams where it seemed as though I was experiencing things from the viewpoint of not one individual but two.

Dreams allow us to easily travel back and forth through the past, present, and future. Locations can evolve and change in an instant, and feats that are not possible in our waking reality—such as the act of flying—can be accomplished in our dreams. All of this makes dreaming the perfect lab or playground for us to experiment and be creative. If we can levitate, possess superhuman powers, and meet fantastical creatures in our dreams, then certainly our dreams should be able to act as a portal for contacting our loved ones who have passed over.

The activities in the remainder of this chapter will equip you with tools to aid in your underworld dreaming efforts. In general, I highly recommend being patient with yourself and setting aside preconceived expectations about what you will experience. Learning to communicate with the deceased can take some time, and often the experience is not what we envisioned it would be. In some cases, the deceased may not be ready to communicate with us, so we must be willing to accept it and be patient with them. Because our subconscious can block our ability to connect with the deceased in an effort to protect us, it can be very helpful to undertake shadow work to identify and heal any unresolved issues, trauma, and fears prior to pursuing communication with the dead.

As with many magickal pursuits, I suggest casting a circle and implementing protective wards prior to underworld dream efforts, at least until you are more proficient or certain that you are communicating with the souls of those who only have your best interests at heart. Loved ones with whom we had a good relationship while they were alive are likely going to be just as loving to and protective in the afterlife. With those we are uncertain of or with whom perhaps we had challenging relationships, it is better to play it safe until we have a better feel for the emotional and spiritual state those deceased are in. In my experience, individuals who were angry or had harmful tendencies during their lifetime do not necessarily change right away simply because they have died. Also, if you are reaching out to an ancestor you have never met and have very little knowledge about, it makes sense to create a protective barrier for all involved as you get to know them better.

Before you do the following activities, think about your purpose for reaching out to the deceased: Do you have a specific question, or do you just want to be in their company for a while? Are there unresolved issues for which you'd like to get closure? Are you searching for general wisdom to help you in your daily life? Having a purpose in mind improves the likelihood that your visit will be successful. For ethical reasons, I don't recommend contacting spirits for trivial questions, nor should you attempt to bring a deceased loved one into your dreams on a daily or otherwise frequent basis. Keep in mind that you are inviting the deceased to enter your dreams, not forcing or pushing them to do so. Even those who have passed over into the spirit world should have some semblance of free will.

SPIRIT/ANCESTOR ALTARS

Many cultures honor the deceased by creating an altar for loved ones who have passed on, be they relatives, ancestors, friends, or even beloved pets. Ancestor veneration is particularly prevalent in various traditions of Asia, parts of Africa, and Mexico. Many consider the term "ancestors" to refer to past generations of one's biological family. This is certainly one category of ancestors, and it can be a rewarding experience to connect with those who have come before you, particularly if you don't know much about them or their lives. Connecting with these ancestors can also help to understand and heal trauma that may not have any identifiable origin. The study of epigenetics focuses on the cellular memory that some scientists believe is passed down through our DNA, which has shed new light on how trauma and fears can be passed on from generation to generation.

Studies have shown that memories associated with fear can be passed down for two generations or more. In research done with mice, scientists found that subjects descended from mice who had been exposed to the scent of acetophenone while receiving mild electric shocks showed signs of fear even though they themselves had not had any traumatic experiences or any previous exposure to the scent.[75] The BBC reports that studies have shown that, "wars, famines, and genocides are all thought to have left an epigenetic mark on the descendants of those who suffered from them."[76] Underworld dream magick can therefore help us to fill in the blanks about what may seem like irrational fears and can promote healing in ways that more traditional methods may not.

However, the category of ancestors is broader than you might think. If you are adopted, ancestors can include those of your adoptive family. Ancestors can also refer to pioneers in a field that you work or are otherwise immersed in. Someone who works in the field of psychology might wish to call on famous psychologists as Carl Jung or Sigmund Freud. Depending on their spiritual beliefs, individuals who follow the path of Paganism may desire a connection to deceased icons such as Victor Anderson of the Feri tradition or Gerald Gardner of the Wiccan tradition.

---

75   Ewen Callaway, "Fearful Memories Passed Down to Mouse Descendants," *Scientific American* website, originally published in *Nature*, December 1, 2013, https://www.scientificamerican.com/article/fearful-memories-passed-down.

76   Martha Henriques, "Can the legacy of trauma be passed down the generations?" BBC website, March 26, 2019, https://www.bbc.com/future/article/20190326-what-is-epigenetics.

Establishing and maintaining an altar for the deceased can enhance your dream mediumship abilities. First, it helps you to focus on what you wish to dream about, and as explained in previous chapters, what you focus on is what is most likely to provide the content for your dreams. Establishing and engaging with this type of altar helps to build or continue a relationship with individuals in the spirit realm much like building relationships in the world of the living; the more you engage with other people, the better you can communicate and the stronger the bonds become. By frequently cleaning the altar and providing simple offerings, you continue to gain the respect of those you are venerating.

A spirit or ancestor altar may be as simple or as elaborate as you would like. Most altars include pictures of ancestors or loved ones as well as items that may have had meaning for them. In addition to pictures, my altar has a watch that belonged to my grandmother and an owl figurine to represent my niece's love of owls. I have heard from multiple mediums that it is not recommended to put pictures of the living on or near the ancestor/spirit altar, as some cultures believe that the dead will be tempted to draw on the life force of or interfere with the living. I personally don't subscribe to this belief because it is not a part of my culture, though I respect and understand it is strongly embedded in other cultures. Before building your altar, you are encouraged to learn more about your own culture's beliefs as they relate to the deceased and any veneration of the dead.

Common items placed on spirit or ancestor altars include but are not limited to:

- Pictures of the deceased
- A glass of water (to be replaced each day)
- Food or other items that the deceased enjoyed while they were alive, such as chocolate, wine, or cigars

+ Items that belonged to the deceased, e.g., jewelry, a handkerchief, or in the case of a pet, a collar

+ A candle (I personally prefer to use a white candle)

+ Something that represents the hobbies of the deceased, such as a spindle for someone who liked to knit or spin wool

+ For ancestors related to specific industries or traditions, you might include a representation of that particular industry or field. It could be a spiritual symbol or item such as a cauldron for spiritual ancestors or a hammer or other tool for an ancestor involved in carpentry, for example

Sitting at your ancestor/spirit altar each day and talking to your deceased loved ones can create a connection that can carry over into your dreams. If you have a specific question or questions, you may want to write them down and place them on your altar. For best results, let them charge there for a few days before you attempt to make contact via your dreams. Sometimes the deceased may visit us in our dreams but may be difficult to recognize or not look like themselves. This charm takes the possibility into account so that not only will we be visited by those we are trying to contact but we'll also know how to recognize them when they appear. It is most effective if made during a waning moon phase.

Charm for Making Contact with the Deceased
Materials

+ Graveyard dirt (ideal if this is from a cemetery in which your loved one is laid to rest, but certainly not required to be effective)

+ A pinch of cinnamon

+ ½ to 1 teaspoon mugwort

+ A small piece of driftwood or wood shavings. (Yew can also
  be used but is poisonous and can be difficult to find in some
  areas. If you use yew wood, I highly recommend doing your
  research first and purchasing it from a trustworthy vendor
  rather than harvesting it yourself unless you are well-versed
  in herbalism.)
+ Frankincense essential oil or a small piece of frankincense resin
+ A small black bag or cloth

Note: The materials above create a general, all-purpose charm
for contacting the deceased. If you wish to make the charm
act as a direct link to a specific loved one, include something
personal from whomever you are trying to contact: a bit of
hair, a perfume they used frequently, a food they liked, a copy
of a small bit of their handwriting, or at the very least, their
name written on a small piece of paper.

Instructions

1. Cast a circle and ward your space as you normally would.
2. Sit across from your ancestor/spirit altar or in another comfortable location where you know you won't be disturbed.
   Open your bag or piece of fabric and place the ingredients
   within. As you place each ingredient in the charm, recite
   the following while focusing on your intent:

   Spirits and ancestors (or the name of a specific person or
   *   pet) I come to you*
   With honor and respect
   And invite you into my dreams
   To converse, to comfort, and to reflect
   May this graveyard dirt provide a link to your realm

*May this frankincense envelop us both in a gentle and
      healing embrace*
May this mugwort help me to be open and aware
*So that I may recognize your presence in my slumber, if
      not your face*
*With this driftwood (or yew) I create a liminal space for
      us to share*
*With this cinnamon I invoke protection, raise my vibra-
      tion and enhance my intuition*
So that my request may come into fruition
You are gone, but not forgotten
You live on in my heart and mind
*With this charm, we bridge the Underworld and
      Dreamworld*
If only for a night, entwined

3. When all the ingredients have been added and you have
   finished the incantation, secure the bag or fabric and place
   it on your dream altar or ancestor altar. When you wish
   to communicate with the deceased in your dreams, hold it
   in your hands while focusing on your intent shortly before
   you go to sleep, and place it under your pillow for the
   evening.

Underworld Dream Incense Recipe

I have used this incense blend when doing the activities outlined
in this chapter as well as prior to going to sleep when doing underworld dreaming. For best results, make it during the fourth quarter
waning moon.

Materials and Ingredients

+ Glass container
+ Piece of jet
+ One part patchouli
+ One part thyme
+ A pinch of cinnamon
+ ½ part juniper or cedar leaves
+ A pinch or two of graveyard dirt
+ Patchouli oil
+ Thyme oil

Instructions

1. In a mortar and pestle or glass bowl, mix the dry ingredients (with the exception of the jet) together.
2. Add 4–5 drops of patchouli oil and 2–3 drops of thyme oil. You may want to add more if you prefer a stronger scent.
3. Once the ingredients are thoroughly mixed, transfer them to your glass container.
4. Put the lid to the container on tightly and shake the container 4–5 times.
5. Add the jet to the container once the incense has been thoroughly shaken.
6. To use the incense, place it on a charcoal disk in a heat-proof cauldron, bowl, or incense burner designed for loose incense.

Guided Meditation: Journey to the Underworld

This meditation is an all-purpose journey to the underworld to invite your deceased loved one or ancestor into your dreams. In this meditation, you will travel to the Greek city of Eleusis, where there is a cave said to be the home of Hades, god of the underworld. According to myths, the cave was the entry point that the Greek goddess Persephone used to travel to and from the underworld. If you ever get the chance to visit Athens, I highly recommend taking a side trip to this city, as it is not very far away. Whereas other Greek ruin sites have restrictions on how close you can get to artifacts, at Eleusis you can actually touch some of the ruins.

This meditation can be done right before you fall asleep or earlier in the day. I recommend casting a circle and warding prior to entering the meditation. If you have not worked with underworld dreaming or related activities previously, I suggest inviting an ancestor or loved one whom you know well and feel comfortable with for your first time.

Pay attention to your breathing. When you are ready, you see a black door in front of you. Although it appears to be solid at first, the door begins to shift into a circular vortex. You walk into the vortex and find yourself on a secluded beach at sunset. The waves are a dazzling blue, and even though the sun is starting to fade, it is still warm.

You see steps carved into the stone face of the cliff in front of you and you walk up the steps with ease. When you reach the top, you see an arid landscape laid out before you. You make your way through the landscape until you arrive at a cave. Directly across from the cave is a pit for offerings. You leave an offering and then turn back to the face of the cave.

Crouching down, you begin to make your way into utter darkness until finally you are able to stand. There are torches on the cave walls and you follow a path downward until you arrive at an underground river. Standing next to the river is a man wearing a black cloak. His face is covered by a black hood and there are a set of keys on a rope tied around his waist. He is holding a wooden staff in his left hand. He holds out his right hand and you instinctively know to take a silver coin out of your own cloak and hand it to him.

There is a small, low black boat on the shore of the river and he motions for you to take a seat. You do so and the man joins you in the boat, pushing it away from the shore. As you glide swiftly down the river, you see what appear to be lost spirits moving around in other parts of the cave. Soon, your guide pulls over onto a bare piece of shore facing two large, ornate doors. Your guide points to the doors and you depart from the boat and head in their direction. When you reach the doors, you prepare to knock but the doors open on their own.

You find yourself standing at the beginning of a carpeted path. On either side of the path are streams of water that abut the wall. The path is lined with torches and at the end of the path you see two individuals seated in thrones. One of these figures is a large bearded man with long black hair and eyes the color of rich amber. Seated next to him is a beautiful woman with emerald-green eyes and long strawberry blonde hair. The man rises from his throne and begins to speak, though surprisingly his voice is gentle and soft in contrast to his appearance. He introduces himself as the god Hades and asks you why you have come.

You explain to Hades who you have come to speak with. You share with him what you left as an offering outside of the cave. He listens intently and then nods to the woman next to him. She smiles and leaves the room. Hades turns back to you and tells you that your request has been granted. Before you can thank him, he places both hands on either side of your head and your world goes dark.

In an instant, you find yourself in a beautiful garden. There is a gentle breeze and you notice that among the lush flora is a pomegranate tree, heavy with fruit. The flowers around you are made of the most vibrant colors you have ever seen, and some even appear to be made of gold. You see in the distance in front of you the deceased loved one or ancestor you wished to visit alongside the woman who was seated next to Hades that you now know is Persephone. Hades lets you know that someone will come to get you when you and your guest are ready to leave. You thank Hades and make your way toward the deceased.

You and your guest find a place to sit and you take a moment to thank your guest for coming. If appropriate, you may provide them with an offering that had some meaning for them when they were alive. Your guest smiles and asks why you have called upon them. You respectfully ask that they visit you in your dream and explain your reason for wanting to commune with them. If there is a specific dream detail that will alert you to the presence of your guest in your dream, your guest shares that with you now.

When you are done talking, you notice out of the corner of your eye that Hades and Persephone have returned. You thank your guest, and Hades tells you it is time to return. After saying goodbye, Persephone turns and walks away with the deceased and you follow Hades back to a door. The door is black and begins to shift, much as the door did in the beginning of this meditation. You thank Hades once again and then make your way within the door's vortex, returning to the here and now. Take a few deep breaths and when you are ready, open your eyes.

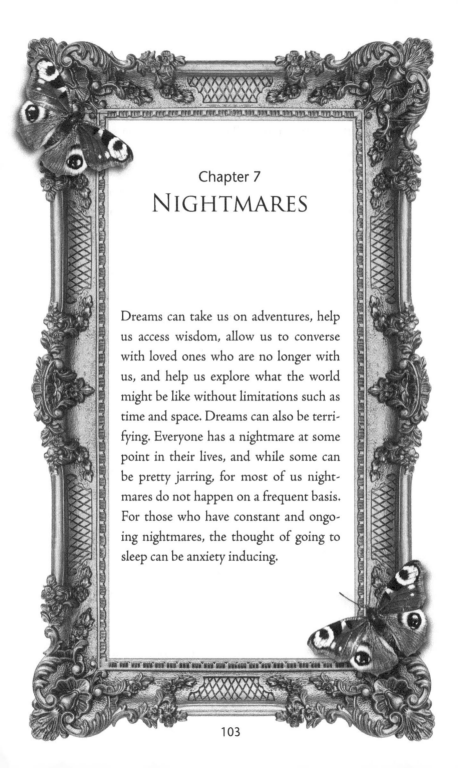

Chapter 7
NIGHTMARES

Dreams can take us on adventures, help us access wisdom, allow us to converse with loved ones who are no longer with us, and help us explore what the world might be like without limitations such as time and space. Dreams can also be terrifying. Everyone has a nightmare at some point in their lives, and while some can be pretty jarring, for most of us nightmares do not happen on a frequent basis. For those who have constant and ongoing nightmares, the thought of going to sleep can be anxiety inducing.

WHY DO WE HAVE NIGHTMARES?

Up to 10 percent of adults have expressed having nightmares at least once a month and often more.[77] Those who have experienced significant trauma seem to be more susceptible to recurring nightmares. According to the National Institute of Health: "Up to 71 percent of trauma victims diagnosed with PTSD have frequent nightmares, compared to only 2 to 5 percent of the general population."[78] Nightmares can have a significant negative effect on our emotions, attitudes, and mindset. Yet, if we are willing to brave taking a close look at these undesirable dreams, they can provide us with very useful information related to our own psychic and psychological development.

If we consider that dreams are messages from our subconscious, then it's not a stretch to believe that nightmares can also provide us with helpful information. They often force us to look at our own shadow elements born of trauma and adversity. Our instinct may be to ignore or try to forget dreams that in some form bring up painful memories, but oftentimes our subconscious calls our attention to these matters because they hold the key to breaking harmful patterns that need to be confronted before deep healing can occur.

Nightmares can be reframed as catalysts for growth but our natural instinct is to avoid things that scare us or we don't wish to see. Unfortunately, that instinctual response tends to make the nightmares stronger and their occurrences more frequent. This is true in general for the things we attempt to avoid. At an Avalonian retreat several years ago, I was participating in journeys in which we each went within to immerse ourselves in the energy of each symbol. The

77   Tuccillo, Zeizel, and Peisel, *Field Guide to Lucid Dreaming*, 183.
78   Katia Levrier, Andre Marchand, Genevieve Belleville, Beaulieu-Prevost Dominic, and Stephanie Guay, "Nightmare Frequency, Nightmare Distress and the Efficiency of Trauma Focused Cognitive Behavioral Therapy for Post-Traumatic Stress Disorder," *Archives of Trauma Research* 5, no. 3 (May 12, 2016), DOI: 10.5812/atr.33051.

journey was designed to help us gain a deeper understanding of the symbols so that we could use them as tools for our own personal growth and healing.

I vividly recall an experience I had with a symbol that represented confrontation and the need to acknowledge and address personal demons. Upon closing my eyes and journeying into this symbol, a terrifying creature began chasing me. I could only get a hazy view of the monster, but it appeared to be a gigantic stag with glowing red eyes and sharp teeth the size of my hand. The panic I felt was immediate and visceral, and I felt an undeniable urge to get away from this creature who I felt strongly intended me harm.

I ran as fast as I could but sensed the creature getting closer. The faster I ran, the faster it ran until it seemed to be mere inches away from catching me. Finally exhausted, I stopped running and slowly turned to face the monster chasing me. The minute I confronted the monster, it morphed into a gentle looking doe and my fear diminished. I realized that the harder we try to run from our shadow aspects, the more insistent they become in making themselves known. By facing them, their power over us diminishes and the frantic chase stops or at least slows down.

Like the creature in my journey, nightmares are messages sent to us from our subconscious in some form not with the intent to harm but to protect, warn, and help us break patterns that no longer serve us. Our subconscious will not be ignored and will continue to make our dreams more startling and terrifying until we pay attention. As daunting as these nightmares may be, it is important to keep in mind that fear of the unknown can be far worse than having to face something undesirable. When we consciously face whatever is haunting us, in many cases we take away its power and remove the need for our subconscious to perpetuate the nightmare.

How to Deal with Nightmares

There have been many proposed methods for addressing nightmares. In *Creative Dreaming: Plan and Control Your Dreams to Develop Creativity, Overcome Fears, Solve Problems, and Create a Better Self,* Patricia Garfield offers options including confronting and conquering the threatening dream image, approaching the dream image in a friendly manner, bargaining with the dream image, finding an ally in a dream to help, and merging with the hostile dream image to learn more.[79] The Sensoi people of Malaysia believed that by asking questions of the threatening images in our nightmares, we can better understand what message our subconscious is trying to give us and thus defeat the nightmare.[80] Here are some examples of questions to ask the images in our nightmare:

- What are you trying to tell me?
- Do you represent an actual person from my life? If so, who?
- Why are you threatening me?
- Can I help you in some way?
- Can you help me? If so, how?
- What do I need to know to overcome my fears so I can heal and move forward?

When it comes down to it, confronting nightmares is another facet of doing shadow work. Therefore, doing shadow work in our waking hours will help us to more effectively understand and dispel our nightmares. However, doing shadow work can be triggering, especially if our shadows have formed from trauma, particularly in childhood. If you have had trauma in your past and are concerned

---

79   Garfield, *Creative Dreaming,* 144–45.
80   Tuccillo, Zeizel, and Thomas Peisel, *Field Guide to Lucid Dreaming,* 189.

about what shadow work might bring up for you, professional help or at least a strong support system before you immerse yourself in exploring past trauma is a good idea, as it can be very difficult and overwhelming. I also strongly suggest being gentle with yourself and trusting your intuition about your level of readiness.

While some dream researchers believe the best way to overcome a nightmare is to kill or eliminate the hostile figure in your dreams, many dream experts (including Stephen LaBerge and Carl Jung) suggest the opposite approach. According to them, the goal is to transform and reconcile the dream figures rather than kill them off. Carl Jung believed that our nightmares or "shadow elements" are parts of our subconscious that need to be acknowledged and accepted. He thought that in order to heal and become more integrated and balanced, we need to accept and integrate the messages that our psyches communicate to us through our nightmares. Doing so not only helps us to sleep better, it also improves our mental health and builds confidence.

Stephen LaBerge has a similar viewpoint. LaBerge advocates "engaging in friendly dialogue" with our nightmares and "entering into a more harmonious relationship with darker aspects of oneself."[81] This does not mean that you have to forgive or become friends with a nightmare figure who perpetrated violence on or other inexcusable actions toward you in your waking life. Frequently the monsters who represent our shadow elements—be they real people or horrific fictional creatures—are stand-ins for elements of ourselves trying to protect us from further harm, although it may sound contradictory.

Having researched shadow work, spoken to others who have studied this phenomena, and done a great deal of shadow work

81   LaBerge, *Lucid Dreaming*, 47.

myself over the past several years, I can attest to the validity of this hypothesis. Intimidating and scary as they may be, our shadows are here to protect us and help us progress and evolve. Nevertheless, their form of protection may seem warped or counterintuitive. For those of us who have been victims of childhood abuse or neglect, our subconscious may have embraced survival mechanisms that worked in those situations but no longer function once we are removed from those environments or when we reach adulthood.

For instance, loved ones who experienced trauma as children told me that the way they were able to survive was to disassociate from the people around them and pretend like everything was fine. By not acknowledging the trauma they were experiencing, they were able to pull through these horrible experiences. Their subconscious perpetuated these coping mechanisms throughout their lives whenever they began to feel threatened, confused, or scared. As you can imagine, these coping methods—while effective in childhood—made it difficult for them to maintain healthy relationships with their loved ones whenever a challenging situation arose.

Is it possible that the frightening figure chasing us in our dreams is actually an aspect of our own psyche alerting us to dangers or wounds that we may not be willing or able to see in our waking lives? Carl Jung and others believe that this is the case and that these aspects of our subconscious and therefore ourselves really just want to be acknowledged, loved, and integrated back into our lives. As poet Rainier Maria Rilke once said, "Perhaps everything that frightens us is, in its deepest essence, something helpless that wants our love."[82]

My own experience with nightmares have confirmed the truth of Rilke's assertion. For many years in both my nightmares and my

---

82   Rainer Maria Rilke, *Letters to a Young Poet*, trans. Soren Filipski (Leipzig, Germany: Hythloday Press, 2014), 50.

waking shadow work efforts, I was haunted by a creature that was too terrible to look at. Over and over, I would find myself entering a dark house with a maze of stairs and hallways until I came to a room in a basement that was lit solely by candles. There, in the corner, was a tall figure with its back to me. It was hunched over and wearing a black cape. I could feel a searing heat emitting from its body, and when it finally turned to me, I could just barely make out a monster that could only be described as the personification of rage.

Each time, I ran from the room and from the house in a panic. When I finally worked up the courage to confront the figure and ask it what it wanted and why it was haunting me, I was stunned to see the figure transform into a version of me when I was a child. With tears in her eyes and a trembling voice, my younger self let me know that she just wanted me to see her, reassure her, and acknowledge wounds that I had never fully processed or healed from. I embraced this younger version of me and let her know that I saw her and I love her. Shortly thereafter, I began to purposefully work on acknowledging and healing these past painful instances that had been affecting me in ways I hadn't previously realized.

Thankfully, these past hurts were not incidents that would be considered significant trauma; they were not born of abuse or intentional neglect, but they were situations that had caused me pain and had contributed to self-defeating patterns without my conscious knowledge. At the time, I thought it was best not to dwell on them, so I moved on without fully considering how they had affected me. I now see that doing so was similar to putting a bandage over a deep cut and expecting it to be fine; while my conscious self moved on, my subconscious never healed. Once I intentionally confronted my nightmare and embraced the scared, hurt child lurking in my psyche, the nightmares ceased.

Nightmare Transformation

While many nightmares feature a villain or pursuer of some kind, not all do. Some nightmares reflect fears, such as accidentally falling from a cliff. Some might involve the death of loved ones, whereas others might replay a traumatic event. The latter type of nightmare is commonly experienced by veterans with PTSD who relive traumatic experiences on the battlefield. Various studies of nightmares over the years—particularly among individuals suffering from PTSD—have found a technique that is helpful in diminishing the frequency of nightmares that works regardless of whether the nightmare's primary characteristic is an enemy intent on doing the dreamer harm or it is characterized by other types of fears. Recording the nightmares is a critical component of this technique wherein the dreamer is asked to re-read the description of the nightmare during waking hours immediately following breathing exercises or other activities designed to help foster a relaxed state of mind. After that, the process incorporates what is known as "imagery rehearsal treatment," in which participants were asked to visualize their nightmare and rehearse a more positive ending at least once a day over a two-week period.[83]

Researchers found that when using this technique, participants' nightmares were essentially "short circuited."[84] One researcher concluded:

> Not only does converting nightmares to "mastery" dreams reduce or eliminate bad dreams, but daytime symptoms of reaction to trauma (i.e., flashbacks, heightened startle response, and generalized anxiety) also tend to subside.[85]

---

83   Rock, *The Mind at Night*, 118.
84   Rock, *The Mind at Night*, 118.
85   Rock, *The Mind at Night*, 118.

The following exercise below builds off the control panel meditation in chapter 3 and incorporates elements of the imagery rehearsal technique described above.

Nightmare Transformation Exercise

You will likely need to do this exercise multiple times throughout the next two to three weeks in order for the transformation to truly take hold in your subconscious.

Instructions

1. Cast a circle or ward as you normally would. It may be helpful to do one of the pre-dream activities in chapter 3 to help you relax and prepare.

2. In a quiet space where you will not be disturbed, recall a nightmare that has been troubling you. If you have recorded this nightmare in your dream journal, notice any consistent patterns that occur prior to having this nightmare. For example, do they occur after specific incidents or on specific days? What is your typical routine the night before you have the dream? Are there any tangible triggers that seem to happen on the day or evening preceding these nightmares?

3. Once you have taken some time to consider these factors, enter the following guided meditation to your personal temple in the astral realm.

Guided Meditation: Journey to Your Astral Realm Temple

Sit or lie in a comfortable position in a space where you are not likely to be interrupted. Start by taking several deep, slow breaths in and out. When you feel sufficiently relaxed, visualize a door in front of you. It can be any type of door or even a portal. When you are ready, step through the doorway and find yourself walking down a pathway through a garden. As you approach the end of the pathway, you find yourself in front of your own personal temple that you have previously visited. The temple may look the same or it may have changed somewhat in appearance, but one thing has not changed—the feelings that you are the master of this temple and the land surrounding it and when you are here, you are completely safe.

You reach into your pocket and pull out the key to your realm. Place the key into the lock and step into your abode. The energy you feel is uniquely yours. It is the energy you feel when you are at your best and feeling happy, safe, and serene. Turn your attention to the picture on the wall that houses your control panel. Consider what, if anything, you may want to adjust on your control panel. Do you feel you need more courage? Would you like to turn down your fear? Maybe you could enhance your creativity to help you in transforming your nightmare. Make any adjustments that you desire to your control panel. When you are done, step out of your temple and into your garden.

In your mind's eye, you see a still image of the beginning of the nightmare that you wish to transform. When you have that image in your mind, project it into an open space in front of you. The image begins to waver as it turns into a portal. You walk through the portal.

On the other side of the portal, you find one of your dream allies. You approach the ally and give them an offering. When they ask what your purpose is here, you tell them that you have come to transform this nightmare to better understand it and give it a more positive ending. You ask your dream ally for any insights or wisdom into the message that the nightmare is trying to give you. Take a moment to listen to what your ally has to say. You then ask your ally if there is any helpful advice that they can give you as you undertake this journey. Your ally responds.

When you are done conversing with your dream ally, you thank them and begin to move forward into your nightmare, re-enacting it up to the point where the villain appears or where something really bad begins to happen. At this point, visualize a different ending. For example, if there is a hostile dream image, you may wish to ask it questions, command it to reveal who or what it truly represents, and approach it with understanding and love. If your nightmare consists of a traumatic event such as a natural disaster or the death of loved ones, you might put things into place that prevent or change the scene. If, for instance, your nightmare consists of you crashing a car, you can choose to drive in a different direction, slow down, or get out of the car altogether.

Continue this re-enactment with a new ending until the dream has ended. Once the dream has ended, take a moment to thank the dream and its characters for sharing their message with you, and state that you no longer need the nightmare as you have acknowledged this aspect of your psyche. You have listened to and accepted the message your subconscious has to offer.

You then walk out of the portal and back into your temple. You walk out through the door and lock it before heading back up the path and back into your mundane reality. When you reach the doorway that you encountered at the start of this meditation, you walk back through and take several deep breaths to return to this reality. If needed, you may touch your hands and feet to the floor for additional grounding.

CRACKING THE CODE

Despite our best efforts, sometimes we cannot crack the code of our subconscious and are subject to nightmares continuing. Working with the Welsh goddess Ceridwen offers an alternative method for confronting our nightmares. Ceridwen's story is believed to have first appeared in written form in the "Book of Taliesin," which is sometimes included as part of the collection of Welsh medieval tales known as *The Mabinogion*. In this story, Ceridwen gathers herbs to create a potion for her son, Afagdu. Afagdu is described as quite ugly, so Ceridwen wished to provide him with divine inspiration (Awen) to compensate for his appearance.

Ceridwen worked on the potion for a year and a day, hiring a young boy named Gwion to keep stirring the cauldron. Ceridwen's intent was for the ingredients to be distilled down to three drops of pure Awen while the remainder of the potion would turn toxic and bleed out of the cauldron and into the earth. Depending on the version of the story, Gwion either intentionally partakes of the potion or—as most are wont to believe—a bit of the potion flies out of the cauldron and burns Gwion's thumb causing Gwion to instinctively put it in his mouth to alleviate the pain.

In either case, Gwion is granted the Awen and is pursued by an angry Ceridwen. She chases Gwion, and they both undergo multiple transformations during the pursuit until finally Gwion turns into a grain of corn and Cerdiwen, transformed into a hen, eats him. As a result, she becomes pregnant with Gwion. Her plan was to kill him once he was born, but when she gave birth, the child was too beautiful for her to kill so she wrapped him up and threw him into the sea. Prince Elffin found the child, who had transformed from Gwion to Taliesin. Taliesin immediately began reciting poetry and making predictions, and he became the most famous bard in Britain.

Ceridwen is a perfect ally to help us in our quest to better understood our nightmares. As her story illustrates, she is able to distill things down to their purest form, leaving the rest of the toxic brew to drain away. By distilling our nightmares into their core message, we can overcome their toxicity and use divine inspiration to help us transform what we fear into things that can help us attain greater self-knowledge and overcome past wounds that may be holding us back in our waking lives.

Guided Meditation: Ceridwen's Cauldron

Sit in a quiet space and take a few deep breaths. You see a door with a picture of a cauldron in front of you. When you are ready, open the door. You find yourself on a path through the forest. To your left is a lake; you see the moon's reflection on the water's surface. You walk along the path until you come to a clearing. You turn to your left and see the lake in the background. A few feet away from you in the center of the clearing is a black cauldron suspended by chains over an open fire. A woman in a black cloak walks out of the forest and stands next to the cauldron. She is stunning, with long silver hair and a face that denotes beauty, grace, and wisdom with just a touch of intimidation. You slowly approach the cauldron.

The woman tells you that she is Ceridwen and she is here to help you better understand your dreams. But, she says, you must commit to the work that needs to be done to quell your fears and heal your wounds. She asks you if you will commit to this work, and you respond that you will. She motions you to move closer to the cauldron and look inside. You see a bubbling liquid that looks like a black abyss. The smell coming from the cauldron is putrid and you begin to question whether or not you are ready for this. Steeling yourself and calling to mind your reason for being here, you look up at Ceridwen and nod.

Ceridwen instructs you to imagine your nightmare. When it is fully formed in your mind, she asks you to project the vision into the cauldron. You do so, and as soon as the nightmare touches the liquid, the cauldron begins to hiss and bubble even more frantically. You immediately step back but before you make it very far, the air stills. Time seems to stop as you notice three green drops rise from the cauldron. In the these drops you can see an image. You step closer, curious, and can make out the same symbol in each of the drops. As you are contemplating what this means, you lift your hand to your mouth. The three drops suddenly converge into one and, now airborne, land on your thumb. Instinctively, you place your thumb in your mouth to alleviate the burning sensation. As you do, your mind is flooded with words and pictures that lead you to an understanding of what the symbol means and ultimately the message your subconscious is trying to convey to you in your nightmares. Take a moment to process the information you are receiving.

Once you have had a chance to make some sense of this new knowledge, you turn to face Ceridwen. If you have any questions about the symbol and this new information, you may ask her at this time. She may or may not answer your questions; know that if she doesn't answer them, it likely means that it is not yet time for you to fully understand or there is self-exploration that must be done first. When you are done conversing with Ceridwen, thank her and leave an offering. Now turn and walk back the way you came, through the door with the cauldron, back to your present reality. Take a few deep breaths. You may touch the earth if you need stronger ground-

ing. When you are ready, open your eyes and record the infor-
mation and symbol you have received.

NIGHTMARES AS MESSAGES

While most nightmares are messages from the subconscious, it is
possible to receive messages from deities during our slumber. Sleep
is a liminal state, and certainly if our deceased loved ones can visit us
in a dream, there is no reason that a deity or other dream ally cannot
visit us as well.

One deity associated with nightmares is the Morrigan, a member of the Irish race known as the Tuatha De Danann.

The Morrigan is the mysterious goddess of war who features
prominently in Irish mythology. Sometimes she is viewed as one
deity, whereas other descriptions of the Morrigan or Morrigna (as
she is sometimes called) describe her as a collective that includes
goddesses such as Badb, Macha, Nemain, and Anu. The Morrigan is
known for providing omens and prophecies. The central story of the
Ulster cycle of mythology, the "Cattle Raid of Cúailnge," has Morrigan visiting the Brown Bull who will fight the White Bull. The Morrigan visits the Brown Bull as a bird and warns him via a poem that
he is destined to be captured if he remains where he is, predicting
devastating future battles.[86]

In stories such as the "Ancient Irish Goddess of War" published
in the late 1800s, Morrigan was said to be able to foretell the death of
men on the battlefield in her guise as a crow.[87] In poems such as "The
Dirge of Fothad Canainne," she appears as the "Washer at the Ford,"
an old woman scrubbing blood from the clothes of fallen warriors as
an omen of death.[88] There is a nuanced distinction to be made here,

---

86   Ravenna, *Book of the Great Queen*, 27.
87   William Hennessy, "The Ancient Goddess of War," Sacred Texts website, https://
      sacred-texts.com/neu/celt/aigw/aigw01.htm. Originally published 1870.
88   Ravenna, *Book of the Great Queen*, 33.

for whereas the Morrigan as a single entity is best known for providing her prophecy in the forms of metered poems, it is in her manifestation as Badb that she shares omens in the form of a crow.

Her prophecies are typically delivered in the waking hours as opposed to in a dream. Yet her alignment as a dream ally lies in the darkness that seems to encompass her and in her ability to shapeshift into a bird—a creature often associated with liminality capable of travel to places that may be difficult or impossible reach otherwise. Devotees of the Morrigan I have talked to shared experiences with wherein they had a nightmare that upon further consideration and communication with the deity turned out to be a warning that helped them avert tragedy or some other undesirable occurrence.

The sources I have explored and devotees I have spoken with seem to agree that the Morrigan is a powerful goddess who should be approached with great respect. She can be terrifying and does not suffer fools, but she also is more than willing to help those she considers hers. The guided meditation here can help you meet the Morrigan and, if she resonates with you, obtain her guidance with any troubling nightmares you may have; particularly any that seem to have an element of forewarning.

As a show of respect, it is a good idea to make an offering to the Morrigan prior to entering into the meditation. I have found items such as Irish whiskey to work well, but don't be surprised if she requires a little bit of blood. (Please note that I am not in any way endorsing injuring yourself to provide her with blood!) I also recommend learning more about the Morrigan to determine whether she is the right ally for you before doing the meditation.

Guided Meditation: Morrigan as Dream Ally

Close your eyes and center yourself with your breathing, counting slowly from ten to one. When you reach the number one, you find yourself on a rocky cliff overlooking bright blue waters. At the edge of the cliff suspended over the water is a bridge made of ropes and tree branches. It doesn't look as sturdy as you'd like, but you get the sense that you must walk across it to the other side if you are to meet with the Morrigan.

You work up the courage to take the first step and, taking a deep breath, you begin your journey. It is windy, and the bridge sways as you make way across, forcing you to hold tight to the ropes. You walk slowly and steadily, with your eyes on your destination as your feet carefully propel you forward. Finally, after several long minutes, you arrive at the other end of the bridge.

Exhaling with relief, you step onto solid land and begin walking through a somewhat bleak forest. You hear a bubbling sound in the distance and soon a stream comes into view. You hear a sharp "caw caw" and turn to find a very large crow perched in a tree, its eyes luminous and wide. The crow flies down toward you and you gasp as it shifts into a woman. This woman is tall and regal, slender but strong, and hair the color of blood cascades down her back. Her eyes, however, look very much like those of the crow. She approaches you but does not say a word. You know immediately that this woman is the Morrigan.

Instinctively you feel the need to bow your head as a sign of respect. You then hold out your hands with an offering. She eyes it, nods, and then points toward a large, flat rock just a few steps away. You place the offering on the rock and turn to face her. She is silent, but the sky isn't. Hearing the clamor of birds, you look up and see that there are several crows looking down at you from limbs in the trees surrounding you.

With the utmost regard for the goddess in front of you, you say her name and ask her for her help with a nightmare that has been troubling you. She quietly stares at you and you feel as though her eyes are looking into your very soul. Finally, she motions for you to follow her to another large, flat rock by the stream. The Morrigan turns to you and asks that you give her your nightmare.

You hold out your hands and envision your nightmare and are surprised to find it manifesting in your hands as a painting. You offer the painting to the Morrigan, and she tenderly carries it to the rock. She kneels by the rock and as she does so, you can hear her singing a somber song but you can't make out the words. You watch as the frame and edges of your painting turn into a battle garment and the colors and images within appear as blood on the garment. As she begins washing the garment in the stream, you could swear that she starts to age. There are gray streaks in her hair, wrinkles emerging on her face, and her body is hunched over. She is muttering something but once again you cannot make out the words.

The blood on the garment begins to fade with each submersion into the ice cold water. When the Morrigan finally pulls the shirt out of the water, you can see that the blood has transformed into pictures, words, and symbols that represent the message the nightmare is trying to convey. Take a moment to look closely at these images. You commit them to memory and, as you do, the garment begins to dissolve until only mere threads are left.

The Morrigan stands, and as she does so, her features once again take on a more youthful appearance. She asks if you have any questions about what you have seen or your next move now that she has helped you to interpret the omen or meaning of the nightmare you gave her. Take a moment to ask your questions. At some point, she indicates that your time with her is up. You ask for one more favor—a symbol so that you may connect with her in the future. She opens your hand, places something within it, and closes your fingers over your palm. Take a moment to look at what she has given you and to memorize this symbol, as it will act as a key for you to return to this realm in the future.

You summon all of your courage to look directly into her piercing eyes and thank her for her help. As the last of your words leaves your lips, she transforms once again into a large hooded crow with wings of black and gray. She looks at you once more and then launches into the sky, flying upward until she can no longer be seen. When you are ready, you make your way back to the bridge but find that this time, the wind has stilled and the bridge is less intimidating. You easily cross the bridge and walk back to the here and now. Take a few deep breaths and when you are ready, open your eyes.

Be sure to record your experiences once you have completed the meditation.

OTHER TYPES OF DREAM DISTURBANCES

While nightmares are common occurrences, a small percentage of the population also experiences night terrors and sleep paralysis. While more prevalent with children, they do occur with adults as well. Night terrors are different from nightmares in that the dreamer typically does not remember anything afterward, including the fact that the night terror occurred. These frightening experiences typically occur in the first to third phases of our sleep stages as outlined in chapter 1 and are characterized by one or more of the following symptoms:

+ Screaming
+ Sitting up in bed
+ Staring with wide, open eyes while technically asleep

+ Kicking and moving wildly about
+ Tendency to sleepwalk
+ Increased respiration, fast pulse, sweating profusely and dilated pupils[89]

Sleep paralysis is a bit different from night terrors and can occur in conjunction with nightmares. Someone experiencing sleep paralysis will not be able to move their body despite attempts to do so. Episodes can be accompanied by hallucinations and difficulty breathing.

There aren't definitive answers as to what causes sleep paralysis, but a French neurosurgeon by the name of Michael Jouvet has come up with some compelling theories. Jouvet discovered that the brain stem experiences what seems like paralysis at the beginning of REM stages of sleep.[90] The suspected purpose is so that the sleeper doesn't get up and physically act out our dreams while asleep, which would be extremely dangerous for them and others. Typically the paralysis goes away when the person exits the REM stage of sleep.[91] However, this is not always the case, as I and others have experienced sleep paralysis upon complete awakening.

In my case, this usually occurred in childhood after particularly scary nightmares. Upon awakening, I would feel like I was being held down by an invisible force and was overwhelmed by panic and fear. The paralysis would usually end after what seemed like several long minutes but was probably only several seconds. Jouvet theorizes that sleep paralysis is some sort of glitch that occurs so that

---

89 "Sleep Terrors (Night Terrors)," Mayo Clinic website, last updated January 13, 2024, https://www.mayoclinic.org/diseases-conditions/sleep-terrors/symptoms-causes/syc-20353524.

90 Belanger, *Dreamwalking*, 150.

91 Belanger, *Dreamwalking*, 150.

the dreamer becomes conscious before the paralysis—the body's built-in protection system—has ceased.[92]

There may not be a definitive cure for night terrors and sleep paralysis, though methods such as cognitive behavioral therapy, biofeedback, and hypnosis have been helpful in some cases. I encourage readers experiencing this sleep disorder to explore these potential treatments. While not a cure, the crystal grid outlined here can provide some protection and peace of mind to help establish a mindset and environment that deters these episodes and assists in helping with the physical and mental symptoms associated with these incidents. Readers experiencing nightmares can also benefit from this grid.

The crystal grid base is the focal point for your grid. You can find simple bases online made of materials such as wood, cloth, or resin, or you can find patterns online and print them on paper. The base typically contains a shape that lends itself to the work you are doing. The flower of life pattern is popular and works well for this grid, as it is good for helping with self-awareness and promoting harmony. Other patterns or shapes that work well are circles, squares, and stars.

White howlite is known to promote peace and help with insomnia. Both black kyanite and onyx can provide protective energy, building a shield of sorts around what you wish to protect. Onyx projects strength and can boost confidence, whereas I have used black kyanite effectively for healing and overcoming energy blockages. Rose quartz is a powerful crystal for easing anxiety, gaining peace of mind, and overcoming fear with love.

In Victorian times, mourners would wear jewelery made of jet to assuage their grief. This stone has other beneficial properties, including dispelling negative energy, purification, helping with anxiety or

---

92 Belanger, *Dreamwalking*, 150.

fear, and providing protection. Obsidian is a similarly powerful stone for protection and purification that absorbs negative energy. For this reason, it is important to cleanse your obsidian between uses. While not required, herbs can also be useful components in crystal grids. Rose petals provide gentle, soothing energy while lavender aids in relaxation. Rosemary is a protective herb and as a bonus can help you to remember your dreams. Finally, the spiky nature of holly leaves as well as its toxicity makes it an ideal protective ally.

Crystal Grid for Nightmares, Night Terrors, and Sleep Paralysis
(Please see illustration following instructions)

Materials Needed

+ Crystal grid base (can be made of any material including wood, cloth, paper, or selenite)
+ Two pieces of white howlite
+ Two pieces of black kyanite or onyx
+ One piece of rose quartz
+ Two pieces of jet
+ Two pieces of obsidian

Optional: rose petals, rosemary, lavender, and holly leaves (Please note that holly leaves can be toxic. If you choose to use holly leaves, be sure to place them in an area out of reach of children or pets).

Instructions

1. Cleanse the crystals you will be using.
2. Place your grid base on a flat surface such as your dream altar or a nightstand. Be sure to place it somewhere where it won't be disturbed.

3. In the outer ring of your grid, place a piece of obsidian in the east and west corners. Place your onyx or black kyanite in the north and south.

4. In between your first layer of crystals, place holly leaves with the point of the leaf facing outward.

5. In the inner ring of your grid, place a piece of jet in the north and south, just above and below the crystals on your outer ring.

6. Place a piece of white howlite in the east and west corners of the inner ring. If desired, place rosemary leaves in the spaces between the jet and howlite.

7. In the very center of your grid, place a piece of rose quartz. In addition to emitting gentle, soothing energy, this crystal also represents you surrounded by protective, healing forces as you sleep.

8. Place rose petals and lavender around the rose quartz.

9. State the intent for your grid aloud and then envision your intent for this grid. Once you have the vision clear in your mind, imagine colored energies reflecting your intent coming up from the ground into your feet and down through your head from the sky. You could use the colors of the crystals in the grid or any color that resonates with the energy you are trying to build. Continue to pull the energy from above and below to your heart center, and then imagine it pouring through your arms and out of your hands, directing the energy into the crystal grid.

10. When you feel that all the energy has entered the grid, quietly focus on the grid for a few minutes. You may then want to ground by touching the floor or stretching a

bit. You will want to re-energize your grid every few days or so, repeating step nine. Be sure to take a moment to focus on your grid prior to falling asleep.

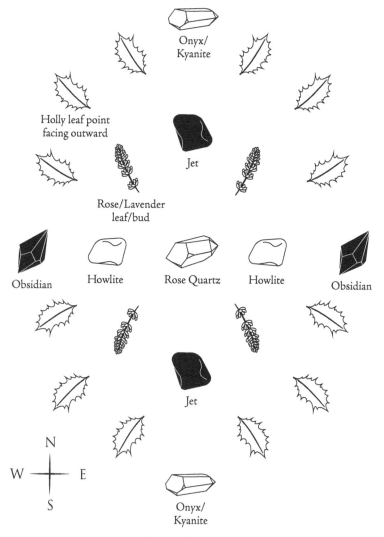

Crystal Grid for Nightmares

Nightmares as Creative Inspiration

Nightmares are undesirable but they can be helpful in some ways. In addition to helping us to better understand ourselves and heal past wounds, they can also unleash our creativity. Numerous writers and inventors have attributed some of their most well-known accomplishments to nightmares. Some examples include:

+ Edgar Allan Poe: The famous author and poet once claimed that the wild, luminous eyes of the woman in his short story "Ligea" first came to him in a dream.[93]

+ Larry Page: The inventor of Google said that the idea for the search engine came out of an "anxiety dream."[94]

+ Mary Shelley: The inspiration to write *Frankenstein* came from a nightmare.

+ Elias Howe: In 1845, Howe had a nightmare in which he was captured by cannibals and told that he must create a sewing machine in 24 hours or he would die. When he was unable to accomplish this goal, the cannibals stabbed him repeatedly with spears featuring a hole at the very top. This led Howe to realize that the sewing machine he had been trying to create in his waking life needed a hole in the pointed end of the needle—similar to the cannibals' spears—in order to work.[95]

+ Robert Louis Stevenson: The author reported that he relied heavily on his nightmares in writing *The Strange Case of Dr. Jekyll and Mr. Hyde*.

Nightmares can also act as cues for lucid dreaming, which is covered in the next chapter.

---

93 Robert Van de Castle, *Our Dreaming Mind* (New York: Ballantine Books, 1994), 15.
94 Carl Walsh, "9 Inventions Inspired by Dreams," Bed Guru website, November 2, 2016, https://www.bedguru.co.uk/9-inventions-inspired-by-dreams.
95 Carl Walsh, "9 Inventions Inspired by Dreams."

Chapter 8
LUCID DREAMING

Henry David Thoreau once said, "Our truest life is when we are in dreams awake."[96] Perhaps his observation reflects why people have been fascinated with lucid dreams for thousands of years. A lucid dream is defined as one in which the dreamer realizes that they are dreaming while still in the midst of the dream. Once full lucidity occurs, the dreamer can consciously affect what happens in the dream.

LUCID DREAMING THROUGHOUT HISTORY

A lucid dreamer who is facing danger can manifest an escape route or

---

96 LaBerge, *Lucid Dreaming*, 7.

change a hostile figure into someone more amicable. Lucid dreamers might also seek information or travel to a place they've never been. Powers and feats that are not possible in our waking lives (such as flying) are easily accessible in lucid dreams. The possibilities existing within lucid dreams are endless.

The first description of a lucid dream dates back to 415 BCE when St. Augustine recorded a dream experience told to him by the Roman physician Gennadius.[97] From the 1500s to the 1700s, philosophers and authors such as René Descartes, Sir Thomas Browne, Samuel Pepys, and Thomas Reid all referred to their lucid dream experiences in conversation, published writings, or journals. However, it wasn't until 1867 that the French researcher Marquis d'Hervey Saint-Denys actually coined the term *rêve lucide* or "lucid dreaming."[98]

Saint-Denys wrote about lucid dreaming in his book entitled, *Dreams and the Ways to Direct Them*. His interest in lucid dreaming was influenced by his attempt to help children get rid of nightmares that had been triggered by traumatic life experiences such as watching a nearby house burn down.[99] In 1913, Dutch psychiatrist Frederick Van Eeden published *A Study of Dreams*, which chronicled more than five-hundred dreams of his, some of which were lucid.[100] Yet it wasn't until the 1950s that dream research began in earnest.

In 1968, Celia Green published her book *Lucid Dreams*, which covered her research into dream awareness and a hypothesis regarding the connection between lucid dreams and REM sleep. The first scientific proof of lucid dreaming occurred in the 1970s and early 1980s as a result of experiments conducted separately by Keith Hearne and

---

97   Belanger, *Dreamwalking*, 140.
98   Garfield, *Creative Dreaming*, 232–33.
99   Garfield, *Creative Dreaming*, 232–33.
100   "The History of Lucid Dreaming–Part 2," The Lucid Dreamer website, http:// the-lucid-dreamer.com/History-of-Lucid-Dreaming-2.html.

Stephen LaBerge.[101] In both scientists' studies, a participant was able to communicate that they were aware of and able to control their dreaming through a set of eye movements that had been agreed to prior to the participant falling asleep.[102] LaBerge opened his Lucidity Institute in 1987, and studies on lucid dreaming continue to this day. Although modern-day studies have provided invaluable insights into the practice of lucid dreaming, there is much to be learned by looking at ancient cultures and spiritual paths that have used dream awareness long before it was recognized by the scientific world.

Two of the most well-known cultural immersions into lucid dreaming come to us from the ancient Egyptians and Tibetan Buddhists. The ancient Egyptians were said to be the first documented society that revered dreams as a direct link to the spirit realm and believed that the soul could intentionally travel outside the physical body during sleep. The common ancient Egyptian word *resut*, whose hieroglyph resembles an open eye, has been translated as meaning "awakening" or "awareness," and use of this word in material dated between 2600 and 664 BCE have led researchers to believe that lucid dreaming was a part of the Egyptians' practices.[103, 104]

Tibetan Buddhists have included lucid dreaming as part of their dream yoga practice, which dates back at least a thousand years. These Buddhists use lucid dreaming as a spiritual tool to achieve enlightenment in part by gaining a deeper understanding of the nature of reality. By maintaining conscious awareness of and

101   "The History of Lucid Dreaming–Part 3," The Lucid Dreamer website, http://the-lucid-dreamer.com/History-of-Lucid-Dreaming-3.html.

102   Robert Waggoner, "Exploring the Scientific Discovery of Lucid Dreaming," *IONS 50* (blog), February 3, 2021, https://noetic.org/blog/exploring-scientific-discovery-lucid-dreaming/.

103   Kasia Szapowska, "Dreams of Early Ancient Egypt," American Society of Overseas Research (ASOR) website, February 2022, https://www.asor.org/anetoday/2022/02/dreams-early-ancient-egypt/.

104   Szapowska, "Dreams of Early Ancient Egypt."

control in their dreams, Tibetan Buddhists can achieve awareness of how similar the dream state and reality can be, as it is the Buddhists belief that both are illusory in nature.[105] While in the lucid state, yogis were instructed to complete specific tasks based on their level of ability. These tasks would get progressively harder and included things like exploring different worlds, transforming into animals, and conversing with enlightened beings.[106]

It is easy to assume that lucid dreaming is a mystical experience beyond the reach of most individuals. Fortunately, this assumption is not correct. Dream researchers Schredl and Erlacher estimate that roughly half of the population has had a lucid dream at least once during their lives and that 20 percent of the population has them at least monthly.[107] There are no confirmed answers as to why lucid dreaming is possible, but according to Andrea Rock, studies suggest that it may be "… the result of physiological shifts in the brain combined with volition and intent developed by the dreamer that introduce an element of self-awareness during sleep."[108] In other words, we become aware of our dreams as a result of a desire to do so and an accompanying change in our brain.

HOW TO ENTER A LUCID DREAM STATE

Lucid dreaming is, therefore, achievable but it does not come without a good deal of experimentation, practice, and patience. The benefits far outweigh the challenges and can result in improved ability, health, and happiness. This has been substantiated not only by anecdotal evidence but also through scientific research. Keep in mind, however, some people should avoid attempts at lucid dreaming, spe-

---

105   Rock, *The Mind at Night*, 8.

106   Tuccillo, Zeizel, and Peisel, *Field Guide to Lucid Dreaming*, 32.

107   Michael Shcredl, Carla Fuchs, Remington Mallett, "Differences Between Lucid and Non-Lucid Dream Reports: A Within Subjects Design," *Dreaming: Journal of the International Association for the Study of Dreams* 32, no. 4 (2022): 345.

108   Rock, *The Mind at Night*, 150.

cifically those who have a difficult time differentiating between what comprises waking reality and what occurs in the imagination and in dreams. Attempts at lucid dreaming may actually cause physical or mental harm to these individuals.

Lucid dreaming has been used effectively in many ways, including but not limited to the following:

+ Motor skill development
+ Diminishing or eliminating nightmares
+ Healing chronic physical pain and other physical conditions
+ Improving mental health
+ Creative problem-solving and learning

The therapeutic use of lucid dreaming has been shown to greatly reduce fears and phobias. Additional benefits include inspiration, self-knowledge, and adventure.

Studies have shown that there are traits that can actually help with this type of dream work. Researcher Jayne Gackenbach has found that lucid dreaming seems to come easier to women, those who meditate on a regular basis, and those who have a highly developed sense of balance.[109]

Stephen LaBerge has found that there are three requirements that are vital to the ability to access awareness during the dream state: the correct application and consistent practice of successful lucid dreaming techniques, strong motivation, and superb dream recall. There are sleep phases that lend themselves to lucid dreaming. Lucid dreaming occurs most frequently during early morning hours when the person is still in a REM stage of sleep.

Apparently, a sleep state that persists for several hours leads to both attainment and successful maintenance

---

109   Garfield, *Creative Dreaming*, 174.

of dream awareness.[110] For these reasons, LaBerge recommends setting an alarm for an hour earlier than you usually wake up. Once you are awake, try staying awake for 30 to 60 minutes before returning to sleep with the objective of having a lucid dream. For example, if you normally wake up at 6:00 a.m., try setting your alarm for 5:00 a.m. and staying awake until 5:30 a.m. or 6:00 a.m. before attempting to go back to sleep. This technique is likely best attempted on a day when you can sleep in longer than you normally would, particularly since it can also increase the duration of the dreams.

The lucid dream tea recipe that follows can assist in putting your body and mind in a state more receptive to dream awareness. Drink this tea prior to falling or asleep. As always, please research the ingredients if you have or suspect you have any allergies, sensitivities, or physical conditions (including pregnancy) that might be adversely affected by ingestions of these herbs. I also recommend consulting a medical professional if you are taking any medications that might negatively interact with these ingredients.

Lucid Dream Tea Recipe
Ingredients

- 2 tbsp blue lotus flower petals
- 2 tbsp chamomile flowers
- 1 tbsp mint leaves
- ½ tbsp butterfly pea flowers
- A dash of orange peel
- A glass jar

Instructions

1. Mix all the herbs together in the glass jar and shake well.
2. Add the orange peel to the jar and shake once more.

---

110   Garfield, *Creative Dreaming*, 155.

3. Place one tbsp of the mixture in a tea strainer and infuse in boiling water. Let steep for 3 to 5 minutes. Optionally, you may add honey or sweetener before drinking.

Knowing how to recognize when you are dreaming is necessary for mastering dream awareness. To start, consider the lucid and pre-lucid states. In a pre-lucid state, you have the feeling that you might be dreaming but you aren't truly sure. This sense can occur quite frequently in your early attempts at lucid dreaming. Occultist Oliver Fox believed that a specific attitude was necessary in order to move from pre-lucidity to lucidity. The four progressive levels of thinking Fox identified in moving from one state to the next were the following:[111]

+ Recognizing dissonance or that something is not likely to occur in reality only after you wake up
+ Recognizing dissonance in the dream but accepting it
+ Feeling astonished by the dissonance in your dream
+ Acknowledging that what is occurring in your dream (while in it) is not possible or is at least very unlikely to happen in waking reality. This thought leads to the conclusion that you are, in fact, dreaming—at this which point the dream can become lucid.

In my experience, it is easier to enter a pre-lucid state when dreaming about something quite frightening, something reminiscent of previous dreams, or when the dream begins to defy conditions of reality, such as being in two places at once or having the ability to time travel. For instance, I have repetitive dreams in which I am driving a car on a narrow, treacherous road or over a body of water, and I am in danger of going off the road. Because these dreams are

---

111   Garfield, *Creative Dreaming*, 154.

repetitive and my mind has been preoccupied with dream work while writing this book, I find myself immediately questioning the authenticity of these occurrences when they happen in my dreams.

A pre-lucid state can take you into a lucid state, but being in a lucid state doesn't always guarantee the ability to influence the outcome of a dream. It is possible to be aware that you are dreaming and remain in a state of observance rather than become an active participant. If you experience this type of lucidity, do not be discouraged. It is not uncommon to have several of these types of dreams in the beginning of your dream work efforts; I have found them to be a positive sign, as they quite frequently lead to full lucidity.

If you haven't had a lucid dream, you might wonder how they differ from ordinary dreams aside from the fact that you are have at least some idea that you might be dreaming. For one thing, lucid dreams can be extremely vivid, with intense colors and sensory input that goes beyond visual. I can attest to reports that the sense of touch, taste, smell, and sound can feel just as real in a lucid dream as they do when one is awake, though that is not always the case. There is also a high correlation between dreaming about things like flying or waking up immediately prior to the onset of a lucid dream.

Keep in mind that while there are commonalities among lucid dreams, we will experience them in our own unique way because the subconscious creates what is seen when we close our eyes. Our emotions, experiences, viewpoints, and beliefs all contribute to the stories that play out while we sleep, so lucidity triggers vary from person to person; what might be unusual for one person in their waking life can be entirely feasible for another. For example, if I have a severe fear of heights and find myself scaling a mountain in my dream, I am more likely to begin to question whether I am dreaming as compared to someone who climbs as an occupation or hobby.

Several techniques can help induce lucid dreaming. From a practical standpoint, you'll want to do what you can to raise your vibration and make your mind more receptive prior to going to sleep, and the pre-dream activities in chapter 3 are effective ways of doing this. Getting into a relaxed state, avoiding substances such as alcohol, drugs, or caffeine, and eating a light meal at least two to three hours before bedtime are all conducive to achieving lucidity. The Crystal Sleep exercise that appears here can also help set the stage for your efforts.

This activity is similar to the crystal grid presented earlier, but rather than using a base made out of wood or cloth, we will be using our bedroom as the base. Crystals have the ability to direct and amplify energy, creating an environment more suited for our dream work objectives. A session of crystal sleep can foster a vibration to align with and intensify our efforts.

Crystals for Lucid Dreaming

Rose quartz is a good heart stone known to ease the mind and produce a feeling of calm. It is also reputed to help foster a good night's sleep. It purifies negative energies and surrounds the person with love.

Moonstones have long been associated with psychic ability and are therefore quite useful in lucid dreaming efforts.

Lapis lazuli corresponds with our third eye chakra, which is believed to be one of the body's centers of intuition. Lapis lazuli has been treasured as a sacred gem in many cultures, and I have found it to be an effective ally in dream creation, direction, and recall.

Amethyst is also associated with lucid dreaming, and it is a very spiritual stone that works well for connecting with the Divine and the higher self, as well as for enhancing astral travel abilities, including astral projection.

Lepidolite is a known mood stabilizer that also has the ability to boost lucidity.

Blue kyanite is a high-frequency stone that facilitates lucid dreaming and psychic ability.

Blue calcite promotes relaxation and a smooth transition into dream states.

With the exception of the rose quartz, all the previously mentioned crystals may be placed on the floor or a stable object such as a dresser or windowsill; whichever space is less likely to be disturbed.

Chakra Points

In this exercise, you have the option of placing stones on each of your chakras or energy centers (depending on your spiritual path). Some beneficial crystals that correspond with the main chakras include the following:

Root chakra: Crystals that are or have red or orange coloring such as garnet, red jasper, and bloodstone. I recommend staying away from crystals such as hematite and obsidian; while they are often associated with the root chakra, their heavy energy may interfere with attempts at lucidity.

Sacral chakra: Orange or red crystals such as carnelian, goldstone, or orange calcite

Solar plexus chakra: Crystals primarily yellow in color including citrine, tiger's eye, and topaz

Heart chakra: Pink or green crystals including aventurine, pink kunzite, and rhodonite. You can also use moldavite, but it is a very powerful stone (technically a piece of a meteorite) that can be incredibly intense.

Throat chakra: Blue crystals such as turquoise, aquamarine, and sodalite

Third eye chakra: Amethyst, labradorite, and azurite all correspond with this chakra

Crown chakra: White or clear crystals such as selenite, clear quartz, and Herkimer diamonds

Because the shapes of stones can be uneven and tend to roll off as we change positions, you might wish to use a string of crystal beads from a craft store, as these can be more easily laid over the body and will stay in position for longer. I typically do not place stones on my energy centers when doing this exercise because I change positions in my sleep quite a bit, but it is an option. Any shape of crystals can be used for this activity, but I find that crystal towers or points are most effective for regulating the flow of energy. The one exception is the center or heart stone, the rose quartz chakra, which should really be a tower for maximum effectiveness though the size does not matter.

All of the crystals used in this activity are designed to raise the vibration of the room and the dreamer as well as foster a lighter energy. Make sure your crystals have been cleansed prior to use, and feel free to add enhancements such as oil diffusers and playing relaxing music. Please keep in mind that anything involving fire or electric heat sources can pose a fire hazard. I recommend using a water-based oil diffuser. If any of the crystals you are using are fragile, put them in a box or some kind of container to prevent breakage.

Crystal Sleep Activity
(Please see illustration below instructions)

Materials needed

- One rose quartz tower
- Two rainbow moonstones
- One lapis lazuli crystal
- One lepidolite, blue kyanite, or blue calcite
- Four small bowls
- Spring water
- Sea salt
- Chakra stones (optional)

Instructions

1. Cleanse the room you are sleeping in so that there is minimal clutter and no dust bunnies under the bed. The space should be as clear as possible so that energy from the crystals can intersect and flow freely.

2. Place a bowl with spring water at the four corners of your room. If you have other doors within your room (such as to a bathroom or closet), be sure to shut them first. Add sea salt to each bowl to absorb any negative or heavy energy that could interfere with your attempts at lucidity. Casting a circle or warding your room is also recommended.

3. Place the lapis lazuli centered at or near the wall your bed is facing.

4. Place your lepidolite, blue kyanite, or blue calcite behind your bed. If this is not possible, place it under your pillow.

5. Place each of the moonstones on a shelf, nightstand, or windowsill to the left and right of your bed

6. Place the rose quartz under your bed directly below the center of your body. This stone acts as the focal stone and conduit for the energies of the other crystals. When you are done, be sure to dim the lighting or turn the lights off completely.

7. Lie down on your bed in a comfortable position. If you are using chakra stones, lie on your back and place the stones on their corresponding chakras.

8. Take a few deep breaths. When you feel relaxed, imagine each of the crystals beginning to light up. One by one, visualize the energy emanating from every crystal except the rose quartz.

9. When all the crystals have been energized, imagine the rose quartz emanating energy in the form of a pink light. The energy reaches up from the point of the rose quartz and connects to the energy of the other crystals to create a grid that rises from the floor and builds upward to the ceiling so that its energies completely surrounds you.

10. Take a moment to state your intention to have a lucid dream. If there is a particular dream you would like to transition into, visualize it for a few seconds.

11. Close your eyes and begin the transition into sleep.

12. When you awaken the next morning, be sure to take the grid down by imagining the energies reverting back into the crystals until the grid is no longer active. Remove the crystals from their locations and pour the water from each bowl down the drain or into the earth to be stabilized and transformed.

13. Document your experiences in your dream journal.

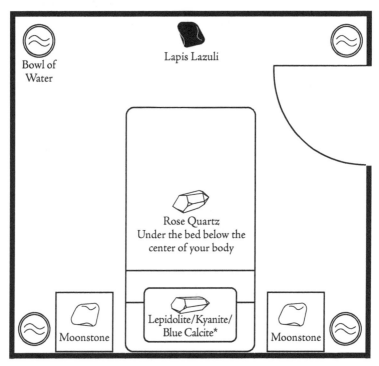

Bowl of
Water

Lapis Lazuli

Rose Quartz
Under the bed below the
center of your body

Moonstone

Lepidolite/Kyanite/
Blue Calcite*

Moonstone

*Under pillow or on a shelf
behind the bed

Crystal Sleep Diagram

Additional Lucid
Dreaming Techniques

Stephen LaBerge is a proponent of what he refers to as the Mnemonic Induction of Lucid Dreams (MILD) technique. In this technique, the dreamer wakes themselves up from a dream (with a preset alarm) and then immediately visualizes themselves being back in the dream before falling asleep again.[112] Another effective lucidity technique that a wide variety of lucid dreamers has successfully used is the "reality check" or "reality test."

Reality testing requires asking yourself if you are dreaming on a daily basis and is especially helpful if you encounter something in your waking life that resembles what you have seen or experienced in your dreams. According to Stephen LaBerge, this must be done at least five to ten times every day.[113] While I agree that the premise of reality testing is valid, I have not found it feasible to stop what I am doing that often during my day to ask myself in all seriousness if I am dreaming. I often forget or get distracted by work tasks or family demands. Fortunately, I have found success in combining LaBerge's reality test with the mnemonic techniques of Robert Monroe of the Monroe Institute.

Instead of trying to remember or intentionally setting aside time each day to do the reality check, Monroe recommends associating the reality check with a specific action or visual cue.[114] For instance, each time you pass through a door or look at a clock during the day, ask yourself if you are dreaming. The premise of both LaBerge and Monroe's technique is that when done consistently enough over the course of many days or weeks, it establishes a habit that will carry over into dreams. As such, when you pass through a door or look at

---

112   Belanger, *Dreamwalking*, 141.
113   Rock, *The Mind at Night*, 164.
114   Belanger, *Dreamwalking*, 144.

a clock in a dream, you will automatically question whether you are in a dream.

However, it is not enough to simply go through the motions of reality checks. You must get to a point where you are genuinely questioning your state of being. One way to make your reality checks more authentic is to actually test your state by trying to perform actions that you would not be able to perform in your waking reality. Some common examples are holding your nose and seeing if you can still breathe, looking in the mirror and attempting to change the color of your hair by thought alone, trying to move the hands of a clock with your mind, or attempting to put your finger through a solid object such as your hand. (As a result of my own experiences, I strongly suggest doing these activities where no one else can see you to avoid misperceptions and awkward questions from others.) You will begin to habitually conduct these reality checks in your dreams to determine whether you are awake or asleep, so be creative in coming up with your reality checks.

Another method for reality testing is to pick an object that is common in your waking life that comes up from time to time in your dreams, even if it is in the background. This object must also be specific and unique enough to actually cause you to pause and notice it in your dream state. Using a symbol such as a building or animal is likely too general to capture your attention. Choosing a more distinct object—such as a barn owl or a two-story house with a wraparound porch—can be common elements in your nighttime narratives and likely to stand out more than something generic or non-specific. To further amplify this technique, take time each day to look at the actual object or a picture of it. The more you concentrate on visualizing this image, the greater the probability that it will show up in your dreams as a prompt to do a reality check.

Stephen LaBerge would sometimes use a simple picture frame as a prompt for lucid dreaming. To use this technique, simply take an empty picture frame and set it on your nightstand or somewhere near your bed. I personally like to use a scrying mirror created from a picture frame—it can easily be made by placing a plain black piece of construction paper where a photo would be. Prior to sleeping, state your intention to become aware in your dreams, and focus on the picture frame while visualizing yourself becoming lucid while dreaming. If there is a specific dream setting that you wish to practice our lucidity in, you can visualize this dream or use a picture or tarot card to represent it. Not only does the picture or tarot card image communicate to your subconscious your desire to achieve lucidity, it also can prompt lucidity if you happen to see its images in your dreams.

The following incense and oil recipes can enhance your capacity for lucid dreaming if used in conjunction with the previously described reality test technique.

Lucid Dream Incense

This incense is most effective if made during the second quarter of a waxing moon. I recommend burning it prior to going to sleep as preparation for lucid dreaming.

Ingredients

- Glass container
- A piece of amber or blue goldstone
- Small pieces of frankincense and myrrh resin
- Small pieces of dragon's blood resin
- ½ tbsp cinnamon

+ 2 tbsp sandalwood powder or chips (Note that sandalwood is at risk of being overharvested. If you are not sure whether the sandalwood you intend to use was harvested sustainably, use sandalwood oil or frankincense as an alternative)
+ 4–5 drops of clove oil (I recommend using essential oil rather than a fragrance oil)
+ 3–4 drops of peppermint essential oil

Instructions

1. Grind the pieces of frankincense, myrrh, and dragon's blood resin until they are in small pieces or fine like a powder. Add the pieces to the jar.
2. In a separate non-metal bowl, mix the sandalwood and cinnamon together, and add the clove and peppermint oils. (Note: The amount of oils in this recipe are a suggestion. I recommend experimenting with the amount of oil so that the scent is at your preferred strength)
3. Pour the herb and oil mixture in the glass jar.
4. Place the lid on the glass jar tightly and shake it vigorously 4 to 5 times.
5. Once it is thoroughly shaken, place the carnelian or blue goldstone in the bottom of the glass jar.
6. Leave the jar under the waxing or full moon for 3 nights. If you cannot leave the jar outside, leave it on a windowsill or near a window, preferably one with a view of the moon. (Be sure to remove the jar before the moon starts to wane). To use the incense, place it on a charcoal disk in a heat-proof cauldron, bowl, or incense burner designed for loose incense.

Lucid Dream Oil Recipe

This oil can be used for anointing yourself prior to sleeping, as it will enhance the likelihood of success with lucid dreaming. Blue lotus and geranium oil are known to aid in inducing lucid dreaming. Patchouli eases anxiety and provides just enough grounding to anchor you in the lucid dreaming experience. Rosemary is an ally in recall, both while in a lucid state and upon waking. Clary sage is a relaxant that also provides clarity. (Many people, including myself, have reporting experiencing a feeling akin to a very slight intoxication upon smelling the oil.) Finally, rose oil adds a gentle yet protective energy.

Be sure to use essential oils rather than fragrance oils. Essential oils are both better for you and preserve the properties and vibrations of the plants from which they are derived. If you wish to use this recipe in an oil diffuser rather than for anointing, omit the carrier oil from the recipe. Keep your oil blend away from direct sunlight and out of the reach of children or pets. Also, be sure to keep pets out of the room when you are diffusing this oil as many oils can be toxic to household pets.

Ingredients

- Dropper bottle made of colored glass (i.e., cobalt blue or amber) to help preserve the oil
- 1–2 ounces carrier oil (I use sweet almond but you can use others such as olive or grapeseed)
- 2 drops geranium oil
- 3–4 drops patchouli oil
- 2–3 drops rosemary oil
- 3 drops clary sage oil

- 4 drops rose oil (neroli essential oil can be used as an alternate if needed)
- 2 drops blue lotus oil *or* 3–4 small pieces of blue lotus flower petals

Instructions

1. Fill the dropper bottle ¾ full of carrier oil.
2. Add the essential oils in the order noted in the above list.
3. Add the blue lotus oil or the 3 to 4 pieces of blue lotus flower (crushed).
4. Put the lid on the bottle. Shake the mixture 4 to 5 times while concentrating on your intent for the oil. On a night that you wish to achieve and sustain lucidity in your dreams, use the oil to anoint the space between your eyes (your third eye chakra) before going to sleep.

If you adapted the recipe for diffusing, simply pour 3–4 drops into your water-based oil diffuser and leave it on while you sleep. (I do not recommend nebulizers or diffusers that do not use water as it can make for a heavier and distracting odor. I also suggest never using anything that requires heat or flame while asleep, even if it has an auto shut-off feature.)

Achieving lucidity can be very exciting, but it is this excitement that can cause a lucid dream to slip away. To be successful in maintaining a lucid state, it is important to find a balance between acknowledging the lucidity and remaining in the dream. The best way to achieve this balance is to remain calm and exercise emotional detachment, similar to the mindset of meditation. Before you take any action, take a deep breath and look around. What do you see? Stay in the role of observer for a few moments.

Engaging your senses in detail can help you to stabilize your lucidity. In his book *The Teachings of Don Juan*, anthropologist Carlos Castenada recalls his mentor, Don Juan, instructing him to "engage his senses by looking intently at his hands whenever he reached lucidity in a dream."[115] While some claim that Castaneda's books about Don Juan were fiction, the methods his mentor supposedly shared with him appear to be rooted in actual accounts of methods for sustaining lucidity. As an extension of the sensory engagement method, Stephen LaBerge found that spinning himself around repeatedly in his dreams upon becoming aware that he was in a dream state helped make his lucid dreams last longer.[116] Maintaining a dialogue with dream characters also helps me cement my immersion into the dream.

LUCID DREAM CUES AND TRIGGERS

The methods shared in this chapter for recognizing, participating in, and maintaining lucid dreams have proven to be very effective in both various dream research studies over the past several years as well as my personal experience. However, these approaches can be overwhelming at times. If you begin to get frustrated or are not satisfied with your results, the best thing to do is focus on being consistent with your dream journal and reviewing it on a regular basis. Doing so will reveal repetitive dreams that can be used as triggers to turn your dream into one where you are an active participant rather than an observer.

Having kept a dream journal consistently for roughly thirty years, I now know that when I am under a lot of stress, I have a tendency to dream about getting lost in an airport (thereby missing my flight), and arriving at Disneyland only to be told that they are closing. In some cases, I am able to get in but my favorite rides—such as

---

115   Garfield , *Creative Dreaming*, 172.
116   LaBerge, *Lucid Dreaming*, 28.

the Haunted Mansion—are a very poor replication of the real thing. (Being pulled around in a little red wagon through a dark, dusty house while adults wearing sheets jump out and say "Boo!" is not quite the ride experience I had in mind!) While these dreams can be stressful, annoying, and disappointing, I now recognize them when they begin and am at the point where I immediately recognize that I am dreaming, thus shifting from a static dream into one where I influence the storyline.

For most people, learning to achieve lucidity in a dream takes time, practice, and a lot of patience. Don't give up if it doesn't happen right away! The techniques for dream manifestation and dream walking in the next chapter can both help improve your lucid dreaming and be fun to try while in a lucid dream.

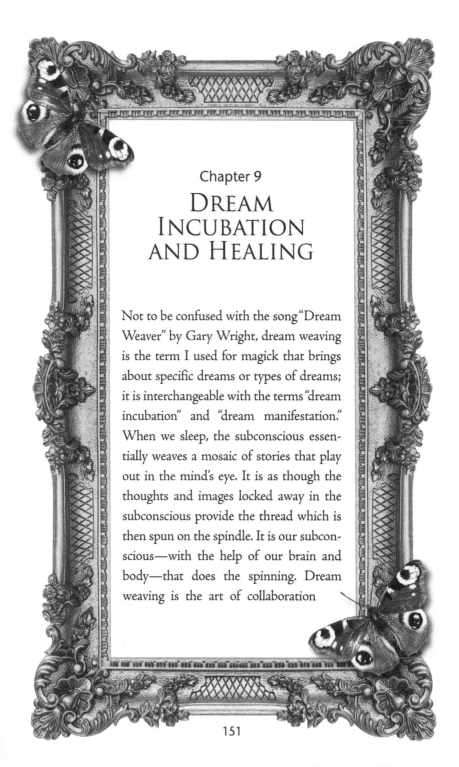

Chapter 9

DREAM INCUBATION AND HEALING

Not to be confused with the song "Dream Weaver" by Gary Wright, dream weaving is the term I used for magick that brings about specific dreams or types of dreams; it is interchangeable with the terms "dream incubation" and "dream manifestation." When we sleep, the subconscious essentially weaves a mosaic of stories that play out in the mind's eye. It is as though the thoughts and images locked away in the subconscious provide the thread which is then spun on the spindle. It is our subconscious—with the help of our brain and body—that does the spinning. Dream weaving is the art of collaboration between the conscious and subconscious minds to create beautiful patterns and luminous works of art that are more intentional than random.

BENEFITS AND HISTORY OF DREAM INCUBATION

Dream manifestation may be best described as a collaboration between the conscious and subconscious minds; while our conscious minds can direct our dreams, it is our subconscious that does the biggest share of the work by selecting the symbols, memories, and visual metaphors that set the stage for a dream. As with lucid dreaming, it can take some effort to create the storyline for our dreams, but there are many benefits to doing so. Many scientists and individuals known for their creative pursuits believe that the way that our physiology works while we sleep actually stimulates creativity. For instance, the artist Jasper Johns was rumored to have deliberately worked with his dreams that resulted in one of his most famous paintings, "Flag."

Accessing creativity in our dreams works not only to aid us in creating artistic masterpieces or inventing innovative things, it also means that our dreams can help us find solutions to challenging problems. Because our subconscious is running the show, we have greater access to all the memories, ideas, and skills we have amassed over our lifetime when we are dreaming. Practicing dream incubation helps us access all these benefits and more, and it sets the stage for manifesting the dreams we desire.

A wide array of cultures throughout history, have used dream incubation, including the ancient Hebrews, Egyptians, Asian cultures, and Muslims. According to Patricia Garfield, formulas for practicing dream incubation have been found in records dating back as far as 3000 BCE from regions such as the Middle East, Egypt,

India, and China.[117] There are theories that even people living in the Stone Age may have retired to their caves or slept in tombs on animal hides in attempts to facilitate dream weaving.

Some of the methods these cultures recorded as well as those of indigenous tribes may seem pretty extreme: rubbing a live guinea pig over one's body, inserting splints under the skin, and sleeping in trees are all dream incubation techniques that have been recorded at one time or another.[118] Fortunately, dear reader, we do not have to go to such lengths to manifest our dreams. Research done on the protocol of the famous Greek dream temples can help us to create a more accessible dream incubation practice.

Belief in the power of dreams can be found in many written records from ancient Greece, and the ancient Greeks as a people were well-known for their dream incubation customs. Even famous philosophers such as Plutarch wrote about successful dream healing attempts. He gives one account of a laborer who was helping to build the Acropolis but fell and was seriously injured.[119] Athens's ruler, Pericles, was upset about the tragedy, as the laborer was not given a good prognosis for survival. Shortly thereafter, Athena came to Pericles in a dream and told him how the laborer could be healed. Perikles followed Athena's instructions and the laborer was cured of his injuries.

Some Greeks conducted dream incubation in tombs, where it was believed that the spirits of the deceased could be found, making it easier for the dreamer to access their wisdom. However, the majority of dream incubation appears to have taken place in temples. Temples dedicated to Asklepios, god of medicine, were found

---

117   Garfield, *Creative Dreaming*, 49.
118   Tucciillo, Zeizel, and Peisel, *Field Guide to Lucid Dreaming*, 208.
119   Tick, *Dream Healing*, 79.

not only in Greece but also in Spain, Italy, Bulgaria, Asia Minor, and Northern Africa.[120]

Asklepios's primary temple was located in a small town in Greece known as Epidauros. Historians assert that dream incubation for the purposes of healing began there around 600 BCE.[121] The Greeks of the time believed that dream incubation could lead to potential improvements in physical and mental health. The majority of dream seekers were likely attempting to find a cure for a physical health condition, but dream incubation was also used for emotional and spiritual healing. The Roman emperor Marcus Aurelius (121–180 CE) believed that the primary goal of medicine was not to cure our physical maladies but to use our ailments to "restore the well-being and integrity of our souls and to unfold our destinies."[122]

Given the stress and turmoil that often pervades our lives, accessing any resource to maintain good mental health is still a relevant concern to us. What happens in our dreams can have a noticeable effect on our mental health and, in some cases, our physical health and our behavior in our waking lives by extension. Furthermore, our mental health and our disconnection from spirit can manifest in physical illnesses, a postulation that underlies the purpose of the dream incubation and healing attempted at various temples throughout ancient Greece.

DREAM INCUBATION RITES

Thanks to the extensive research done by historians, archaeologists, and other scientists, we have a good deal of information about what exactly occurred before, during, and after dream incubation. While there were multiple dream temples ascribed to different deities,

---

120   Tick, *Dream Healing*, 5.
121   Tick, *Dream Healing*, 6.
122   Tick, *Dream Healing*, 215.

the temples dedicated to Asklepios were some of the most popular. Ancient Greeks would travel far and wide to seek dream cures from the god of healing himself or through the snake that appeared on his healing staff. Much like the Greek Eleusinian mysteries, the practice of dream healing surpassed class roles.

Whether at the highest level of society or the lowest, every entrant would shed their clothing and their status in the outer world; no one was given special instructions that deviated from the ones given to other dream seekers due to a high standing in society. For the most part, all seekers at Asklepios's temples followed the same procedure: purification via a ritual bath, donning a white robe upon emerging from the bath, and presenting themselves to the temple's priests. In some cases, sacrifices were made to appease Asklepios and attain his favor.

After a visitor presented themselves to the priests, the latter would determine if the individual was in a receptive state of mind prior to beginning the incubation. Any individual deemed not ready would be sent away and instructed to return another day. If the seeker was ready, they would be led into the *abaton*, the temple's sleeping chamber. The dark chambers within the abaton were narrow and womb-like, an intentional design that represented a descent into the subconscious and a return to the origin of the person's wounds.[123]

In some instances, dreamers slept on animal hides or were wrapped tightly in bandages that would be removed after their incubation period was complete.[124] The seeker would attempt to sleep in the chamber and stay there for as long as it took to receive a healing dream. If they were successful, Asklepios would take the form of a human, snake, or dog, and come to the seeker in their dreams to

123 Tick, *Dream Healing*, 30.
124 Caitlin Matthews and John Matthews, *The Encyclopedia of Celtic Wisdom* (Rockport, MA: Element Books, 1994), 334.

either cure them or would provide medical advice relevant to their condition.

Pergamum (modern-day Bergama in Turkey) is one of the most famous healing centers associated with Asklepios and dream incubation. An inscribed fragment found there is said to hold the clues to an ancient dream healing ritual. Author Edward Tick provides the following elements for a dream incubation ritual: [125]

+ Purification with water
+ Dressing in a pure white tunic and wearing garlands of olive shoots. Dreamers may not wear any other accessories such as belts or jewelry, and they must be barefoot.
+ Transition to a liminal space so that the dreamer could feel as if they were leaving mundane time as they entered the sanctuary. Once the dreamer entered the abaton, they would spend an extended amount of time there—sometimes up to ten days—to separate themselves from their daily reality.
+ The dreamer may have been subjected to dietary changes that could include abstinence from certain types of food as well as fasting.
+ Participation in further purification activities such as ritual baths, saunas, and steam baths. It also included celibacy and participation in meditation and long periods of silence.

All of these dream incubation elements were intended to change a person's body chemistry and disrupt space and time in order to induce an altered state of consciousness. If the dreamer was not able to interpret their dream, one of the priests would assist in providing clarity.

---

125   Tick, *Dream Healing*, 164.

HEALTH BENEFITS OF DREAM INCUBATION

While it may seem like a fantastical and perhaps ineffective process for healing, there is historical documentation that seems to point to the effectiveness of dream incubation. Many inscriptions have been found bearing recorded dream incubation cures dating back to the fourth century BCE at the site of Asklepios's temple in Athens. Famous Greek author and philosopher Pliny the Elder asserted that Hippocrates, the father of medicine, learned the healing arts by writing down and studying cures recorded by dream incubation participants at one of Asklepios's temples.[126] In addition to providing cures, incubated dreams can alert us to physical conditions that we may not be consciously aware of.

There is some scientific backing for the premise that dream incubation can be of great benefit. Dreams provide us with visual imagery, and studies have shown that our bodies don't distinguish between intentional visualizations and actual events. Various medical institutions and organizations including the Mayo Clinic and John Hopkins Medicine have attested to the fact that guided imagery can help mitigate symptoms for a variety of ailments such as allergies, diabetes, heart disease, and carpal tunnel syndrome.

Dr. O. Carl Simonton, a cancer researcher and radiation oncologist, conducted a study of the effectiveness of visual imagery in helping to heal cancer patients. He reported that patients with advanced cancer who used visual healing imagery in conjunction with radiation and chemotherapy survived on average twice as long as national averages predicted for their condition.[127] Studies have also shown that people under deep hypnosis can in some cases exert control over some bodily functions, such as changing their heart rate or rate of breathing, and

---

126   Tick, *Dream Healing*, 90.
127   LaBerge, *Lucid Dreaming*, 34.

slowing or stopping bleeding. Because our subconscious is not constrained by the limitations of our waking world, it is reasonable to assume that these same changes can be made in a dream state.

Creating a Dream Incubation Temple

The following activity provides some basic guidelines for setting up a dream incubation temple and ritual on the physical plane. Activities presented later in this chapter will reference dream temples created on the astral plane, but having a physical space that can be used for dream incubation is beneficial, especially if you are new to the practice. The guidelines for creating your dream temple are just that—guidelines. Use your creativity to make this space your own. Having a special room dedicated for dream incubation can be helpful, as your mind will associate it with dream magick and your unique energy will be strongly felt after sustained use of your temple, However, it may not always be possible or practical to set aside a separate room or space to use as a permanent dream temple and that is fine. The elements of ritual and how you set up your space when you use it will be the key to putting your mind into the state of receptiveness necessary for dream magick to work.

The intent in creating a dream incubation temple is to establish a sacred space for manifesting dreams which include but are not limited to dream healing. When I use my dream temple, I dim the lights and create a circle with candles. (I suggest using flameless candles or other lighting as you will be in the space for some time, and you don't want to worry about knocking them over or starting a fire. Light sources will be turned off prior to sleeping; you will be in utter darkness during your dreaming.)

Burning incense and casting a circle are two ways in which I set the space apart as being sacred and settling my mind into the work ahead. Your dream temple should be as uncluttered and clean as possible in order to assure good flow of energy. I also like to play shamanic drumming or other spiritually-themed music at a low volume to help induce a trancelike state. Incorporating statues or representations of dream allies and dream magick in general can add to the energy in this space.

As mentioned previously, the rooms and tombs that dreamers would sleep in were very dark, and it was not uncommon to sleep wrapped up in bandages or animal hide. To create a similar experience, I suggest using a weighted or heavy blanket to wrap yourself in. I also find it helpful to use an eye pillow, or a small, simple pillow filled with rice placed over your eyes. I recall reading once that while performing imbas forosnai (prophetic magick), druids would place stones over the eyes to shut out any sensory input. While unfortunately I don't recall where I read this, I can tell you from my own experience that placing something lightweight such as a pillow over the eyes seems to help the mind shift more rapidly into a state conducive to dream incubation and prophecy.

Once your dream temple is set up, use the following ritual for dream incubation. (Note: You can do this for yourself or act as a dream proxy for someone else as long as you have their permission. If you are acting as a proxy, be sure to clearly state who you are lying in for and what they have requested.)

Dream Incubation Ritual for Healing
Materials

+ Flameless candles or other dim lighting
+ Lighter
+ Incense
+ Robe or other comfortable garment
+ Weighted or heavy blanket

+ Eye pillow or sleep mask
+ Pillow for your head
+ Flash paper and pen, plus cauldron or heatproof container
+ Music (optional)
+ Source of white noise (optional)
+ Dream journal and something to write with
+ Dream herbs and oils for a ritual bath
+ Water and a light snack

Instructions

1. Purify your dream temple space through whatever method most resonates with you. You can use sound, sacred smoke, asperging, and using energy modalities. Turn off your phone and other electronics to ensure you won't be interrupted.

2. Leave your dream temple and go take a ritual bath in silence using one or more of the dream herbs or oils listed in appendix C. Feel free to use candles as well to create a relaxing ambiance. Close your eyes and take some time to experience being "held" in a liminal space by water.

3. When you are done with your bath and have dried off, wrap yourself in a robe or other comfortable garment. Make your way to your temple in silence. (At this step, I suggest bringing water and a snack with you in case you need some grounding once you wake up. You will also want to bring your dream journal and something to write with).

4. Standing in the middle of the room, cast a circle in your dream temple.

5. Light candles and incense and do any other preparations needed to make your temple fully ready.

6. Sitting in the center of your circle, prepare your sleeping space including your blanket, pillow, and whatever you are using to cover your eyes—eye pillow, sleep mask, or even a dark, thin scarf.

7. Visualize your intent for healing. Be clear about any condition you wish to learn more about and heal. You could also ask to be shown any medical conditions or vulnerabilities that you are not aware of. State this intent out loud. Write the intention (and the name of the person you are sitting in for if you are a proxy) on a piece of flash paper. Over a cauldron or other heatproof container, burn the flash paper. This will symbolically "send" your intent to the dream world immediately.

8. Take some time to meditate and sit in silence.

9. When you are ready, extinguish any candles, lighting, and incense. Be sure to turn off any music if you think it will interfere with your sleep. If you do choose to sleep with music on, be sure it is instrumental only and not jarring in any way. If you are worried that other noises in your environment could be distracting, white noise may be the best option, either in an online video or playlist, or with a machine. While white noise is most effective with headphones, but can be used without them.

10. Lay down in a comfortable position and wrap the blanket around you. Placing the eye pillow or sleep mask over your eyes, close your eyes and take ten deep breaths while thinking about your intent. Continue to state your intent and think about your intent as you drift off to sleep.

11. Any time you awaken, record your dreams in your journal. When you are done sleeping, release the circle you have

cast. Be sure to drink some water and eat some food if you are feeling light-headed.

12. Later in the day, look at your dream journal to see if you can find any evidence of healing or medical information being given. If you acted as proxy for someone, be sure to share any information.

It may take some time to interpret your dream and you may have to repeat the process more than once before you get the information or healing you desire.

ADDITIONAL METHODS AND ADVANTAGES OF MANIFESTING DREAMS

Practicing dream incubation can make our waking lives more fulfilling, a belief shared in various cultures throughout history. What's more, not all dream manifestation rituals occurred in a temple. In her book *Celtic Visions*, Caitlin Matthews references a traditional Scottish dream weaving ritual once used to locate missing people.[128] When a ship did not return home, "…a virgin woman of strong mind was asked to sleep and send out her spirit to seek for its whereabouts…Her dream report on waking could send rescuers to discover the wreck or any survivors."[129]

Thankfully, dream manifestation can be done in many different ways regardless of whether we have a physical dream temple or we follow the prescribed steps as given to us by the ancient Greeks. There may be occasions when we don't have access to a tangible sacred dream space and we may not have the time or ability to follow a full dream incubation purification rite and ritual. As

128   Caitlin Matthews, *Celtic Visions: Seership, Omens, and Dreams of the Otherworld* (London: Watkins Publishing, 2012), 39.
129   Matthews, *Celtic Visions*, 39.

mentioned in a previous chapter, people who have vivid imaginations tend to have an aptitude for dreamwork. It makes sense, then, that our imagination would be one of the keys to unlocking the mysteries of how our dreams are created in the first place. Creative visualization can form the basis of an effective dream manifestation practice.

When we are deep in our imagination, the experience is similar in some ways to a dream in that it can be disorienting. Have you ever been so wrapped up in a daydream so lifelike and absorbing that in the moment it was almost as if the things happening around you cease to exist? If we can create such a strong experience just using our mind's eye during our waking hours, there is no reason why we can't create and visualize something just as powerful in our dreams.

In order to maximize the effectiveness of visualization, we must also immerse ourselves in our desired dream subject as much as possible, right up until the moment we fall asleep. We have already learned that conscious thoughts can have a huge impact on our dream content. As Patricia Garfield points out, "Intense occupation with any subject is likely to induce dreams of it."[130]

As noted previously, the brain reacts the same way to thoughts as it does to actual occurrences. In one study, a group of athletes underwent an electromyography (EMG) that measures electrical impulses in the body. The study found that the electrical impulses these athletes had were the same whether they were doing an activity or simply thinking about it.[131] Creative visualization and mental immersion in what we wish to dream about are critical, yet a third element is also required to achieve success—intent.

Dream weaving is a lot like spellcasting: we need to be very clear about our intent and express it, usually aloud. The stronger

---

130   Garfield, *Creative Dreaming*, 63.
131   Tuccillo, Zeizel, and Peisel, *Field Guide to Lucid Dreaming*, 54.

our emotions and our desire are in our dream weaving efforts, the greater chance that we will attain our goal. This can also help our memory of the dream to be stronger as well. Finally, the more likely we have faith in our efforts and expect that a positive outcome will occur, the more likely that our dream weaving efforts will bear fruit.

Programming a Crystal for Dream Manifestation

A very simple method for manifesting a specific dream is to program a crystal. A clear quartz works best for this purpose. Be sure to cleanse the crystal before you charge it with your intent.

1. First, create on your intent. Writing this intent down is vital for clarity and conciseness. Using positive language, write what specifically you wish to dream about, visualizing it in your mind as you do so.

2. Hold the crystal in your right hand as you gaze into it. Clear your mind as much as possible.

3. While holding the crystal in your hand, read your intent out loud three times, followed by the statement "As I will, so mote it be" or some variation thereof.

4. Visualize your dream in your mind's eye. When you can see it as clearly as possible, imagine the visualization being projected into the crystal. If you have a difficult time visualizing, you can also use your other senses, such as hearing and touch. Home in on the sounds or feelings that your dream will evoke and imagine those going into the crystal as well.

5. Once you have completed sending your dream and intention into the crystal, imagine energy rising from the earth and descending from the sky into your body. Focus the energy into your right hand, and visualize the energy from your hand building in intensity.

6. When you feel that the energy in your right hand has sufficient power, imagine it surrounding your crystal as well as filling the crystal up.

7. Place your crystal on your altar to charge it. You can renew or increase its charge by placing it under a full moon or setting it on or near a piece of selenite.

8. When you are ready to manifest your dream, place the crystal near you or under your pillow. You can also hold on to the crystal as you fall asleep, but you may have to search for it once you awaken.

Crystal programming is most effective when you have a clear vision for your dream. But sometimes, we don't know specifically what we wish to dream about—that is, we don't have a full story outlined in our minds. Often, we may have a subject in mind with the hopes of obtaining information, finding creative solutions, or getting insights into a particular challenge. We can essentially set the tone or theme of and purpose for the dream we wish to have and let our subconscious fill in the rest. These types of dream work efforts also require creativity, clear intent, and intense passion to find the answers in the dreams we weave.

The following activities help with dream weaving. The first is a ritual to set your intent and to immerse yourself in your chosen topic prior to going to bed. The second can be used separately or in conjunction with the ritual. Committing to a regular meditation practice can greatly aid these and other dream work activities. For optimal success, keep in mind that while they aren't requirements, variables such as moon phases and seasons can amplify dream work, adding an added layer of power to your efforts. For instance, spring and summer may be more aligned with dreams about relationships and fertility/

abundance, whereas dreams centered around shadow work or discovering potential adversaries may be clearer in the winter months.

Dream Weaving Ritual

This is best done during a waxing or full moon.

Materials

+ Two long cords or long pieces of yarn in black, dark blue, or silver or any combination thereof

+ One colored cord or long piece of yarn to represent the intended topic of your dream. (e.g., green for finances, red or pink for relationships, yellow for friendship, light blue or white for health issues, and so on)

+ One candle each to represent the four directions: north, south, east, west

+ One element to represent each of the directions (i.e., water, incense for air, another candle for fire, and salt or soil for earth)

+ A visual or symbolic representation of any dream guide or deity you wish to assist you in this ritual and spell. You could also use a separate candle to represent deity, a dream ally or guide, and the element of spirit

+ Written intention statement

Instructions

1. Cast a circle as you normally would.

2. Purify your working space within the circle using your preferred method. Sacred herbs, blessed water, energy modalities such as Reiki, or sound (chanting, bells, and crystal singing bowls) are all good options.

3. Light the candle in the east as you say the following:

Blessed east, element of air
Ever moving, your night sky shining bright
May your winds carry my dream to me
As I will, so mote it be

4. Light the candle in the south as you say the following:

   Blessed south, element of fire
   Bring me that which I desire
   May your spark ignite the dream I wish to see
   As I will, so mote it be

5. Light the candle in the east as you say the following:

   Blessed west, element of water
   May your waves carry me to the dream I seek
   By your power may I dream with clarity
   As I will, so mote it be

6. Light the candle in the north as you say the following:

   Blessed north, element of earth
   Giver of life, from the seeds I plant
   May you nurture my dream so it will blossom for me
   As I will, so mote it be

7. Face your representation for your deity, dream ally or guide, or the element of spirit. Ask for their blessing and assistance in a way that feels right to you.

8. Sit in the center of your circle. When you have settled in a comfortable position, read your intention statement with deep faith and passion. If possible, try to engage as many of your senses as possible as you image that your desire has

been fulfilled and will be ready and waiting for you once you fall asleep.

9. Take your three pieces of yarn or cord in your hands and tie them together at the very top, with the color specific to your desired dream in the middle.

10. Begin braiding or weaving the three pieces of yarn together. As you do so, focus on your intended dream. You may even want to read your intention out loud as you do so. When you are done braiding the yarn together, read your intention out loud one more time with great intensity. Imagine that you send energy into the braid.

11. Tie the ends of the yarn together (similar to step 9) as you chant the following:

By my will divine
This dream is mine
While I sleep
This dream will keep
Answers clear, with nothing to fear
I receive the dream that I hold dear
As I will, so mote it be
Chant the spell and be it done

12. Thank your deity and dream guide or ally for their help. Then, starting with the north and working counter clockwise, put out the candles and thank the elements for their help one by one.

13. Close your circle. While it is not necessary, you may want to put the dream braid on your dream altar or under the moon to charge for a few nights to boost its power. When you are ready to use the braid, simply place it under your pillow

before you go to sleep. You may leave it there for more than one night if the first night you use it is not successful.

14. When you are done using your braid, untie and unwind the pieces of cord or yarn. If you wish to use these pieces of yarn or cord again for a different dream, be sure to cleanse them via whatever method you prefer: passing them through incense smoke or the smoke of sacred herbs, using energy modalities such as Reiki, and so on.

DREAM PORTALS

The portal meditation is a great way to manifest a dream about a specific topic. I generally choose to use colors to mark the doorway or portal that I wish to enter. For example, if I have questions about my health, I might use a light blue door. Doors with red or pink are associated with passion and love. If you are having a hard time stepping into your dream once you have entered the doorway, you can also use imagery from a tarot or oracle card that corresponds with your dream intent. When I have wanted to manifest a dream about the future of my desired career or future job, I have visualized the Eight of Pentacles card appearing immediately upon opening a green door. If I am trying to get clarity about a conflict, I will visualize the scene in the Five of Swords.

Here are the correspondences for each tarot suits:

+ Pentacles (Earth): Finances, careers, fertility, material objects

+ Cups (Water): Relationships, emotions, intuition, healing

+ Wands (Fire): Action, creativity, transformation/growth, travel, will, finding purpose

+ Swords (Air): Communication/expression, choices, personal power, education, logic

In some traditions, wands are connected to air and swords to fire. Use whatever correspondences fit your path and feel right to you. You can also use major arcana cards as dream imagery, especially for significant life decisions or when you are at a major crossroads. When selecting a card, I recommend trusting your intuition. Remember that the language of your subconscious is unique to you, so it is best to use whatever imagery you feel most drawn to when attempting to manifest a specific dream.

The dream self mentioned in this meditation is similar to an astral projection of yourself. Dream travels are thought to be a form of astral projection, and when we travel during our sleep, our physical body reunites with our astral body shortly before or upon waking. When the term "dream self" appears in the meditation, it simply refers to the astral part of you that travels through your dreams each night as you sleep. This meditation is best done shortly before sleeping so that your dream self is not separated from your physical body any longer than necessary.

Portal Meditation: Dream Manifestation

Note: This activity can be combined with the Dream Weaving ritual and spell. If you wish to combine them, be sure to do the meditation immediately before beginning to weave your dream braid. You can also alter the meditation to use the astral temple established in chapter 3, as opposed to the astral temple described here, which is used solely for dream magick.

Get in a comfortable position and breathe in and out for ten slow, deep breaths. When you are ready, imagine in your mind's eye that you are in a forest at night. In front of you is a locked gate. You search in the pocket of the cloak you are wearing and pull out a key. You find that the key is a perfect fit for the gate's lock. You open the gate and lock it securely behind you.

The air around you is both enchanting and odd. The trees seem to bow toward you ever so slowly and the sky seems to almost be gently moving and swirling as though it is doing a dance. You take ten steps forward and, as you emerge from the forest, you see ten steps made of rock in front of you that spiral and lead downward. You cannot see what lies at the bottom of these steps, but you know you are meant to take them. With only the stars and the smallest slivers of moonlight to guide your way, you begin descending the staircase. Count each step as you take them. As you continue, think about the dream you wish to manifest and any questions you wish to have answered in your dream.

When you finally get to the bottom of the stairs, you find yourself on a beach. Several steps ahead of you is a body of water surrounding a beautiful ancient castle. The castle appears to be made out of the night sky and moon itself, and you notice candlelight in the castle windows flickering almost like stars and walls that seem to emit a silvery glow. You walk to the edge of the water that prevents you from reaching the castle. You are confused at first: you know you are supposed to enter the castle, but you don't know how to get across the water. You think for a moment and quietly state your intent to yourself to enter the castle for the purpose of dream manifestation. Slowly but surely, a bridge appears in front of you.

You begin to walk across the ten steps of the bridge. Each time you take a step forward, the plank that you are no longer standing on fades away such that by the time you get to the castle grounds, the bridge is gone. Taking out the key from your cloak again, you slip it into the lock and the door to the castle opens with a creak. You immediately feel a welcoming energy and know that this place was destined to be claimed by you for your use only.

You walk into the center of the foyer, which is lit by the waxing moon overhead. Straight ahead, you see a door at the other end of the foyer, lit from within by a silvery light. You walk to and open the door. Once you set foot in the room, it closes softly. Ahead of you is a set of three doors. You look to the door in the middle as you state your intent for dream weaving. As you do, the color of the door shifts to correspond to your intended dream topic. The door does not open, however, it acts as a portal.

As you move toward the door, you see your dream self—a perfect replica of you in every way—separate from your body. You once again state the intent of your dream with full confidence that this dream will occur during this evening's sleep or soon thereafter. Your dream self smiles, and you look down to find a silver yarn connecting the two of you. You tell your dream self that the yarn will keep you connected and that they are to return to your physical body upon waking in the same way during a normal course of sleep and accompanying dream travel. You also advise your dream self to remember the content of this dream and integrate it into your conscious mind to make dream recall successful. Your dream self nods and then turns to walk through the portal.

Since you are still connected and can cross the portal, you have the option to imagine tarot or other imagery on the other side of the door. When you are ready and feel that your dream self is well positioned on the other side of the door, walk back into the foyer and out of the castle. The bridge materializes again as you step to the edge of the water. You walk across the bridge and over to the shore, where you ascend the stairway. You then walk back through the forest and through the gate, unlocking and then relocking it as you did before. When you are ready, walk back to the here and now. Take a few deep breaths and, if needed, ground yourself by touching the floor or having a small bite to eat prior to going to sleep.

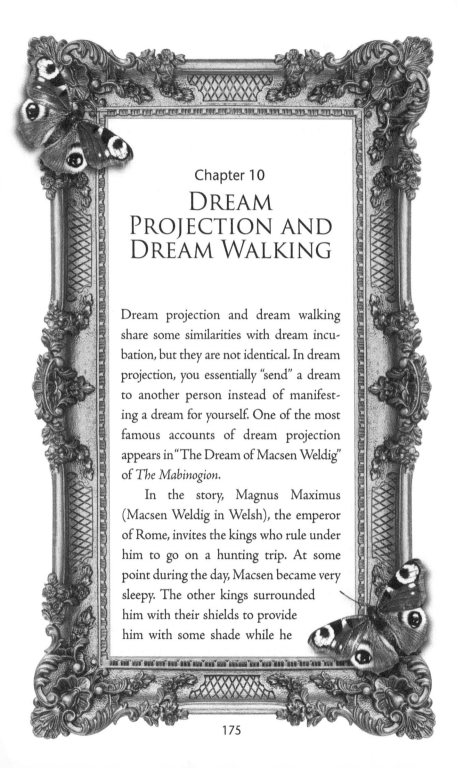

Chapter 10

DREAM PROJECTION AND DREAM WALKING

Dream projection and dream walking share some similarities with dream incubation, but they are not identical. In dream projection, you essentially "send" a dream to another person instead of manifesting a dream for yourself. One of the most famous accounts of dream projection appears in "The Dream of Macsen Weldig" of *The Mabinogion*.

In the story, Magnus Maximus (Macsen Weldig in Welsh), the emperor of Rome, invites the kings who rule under him to go on a hunting trip. At some point during the day, Macsen became very sleepy. The other kings surrounded him with their shields to provide him with some shade while he slept. As he slept, he had a dream that he went on a great journey that ultimately led him to a river. The land was extraordinary, and he saw a castle at the mouth of the river. When he entered the castle, he saw that it appeared to be made of the finest gold and precious jewels. In the hall, he saw two auburn-haired boys playing chess on a silver table with gold chess pieces. The young boys were wearing clothing also comprised in part of jewels and gold.

Next to a pillar in the hall, Macsen saw a large muscled man who looked wild and disheveled in appearance. Unsurprisingly, the man was also wearing gold, including a diadem, bracelets, and a torc. The man appeared to be carving chess pieces for the young boys to play with. What dazzled Macsen the most was a beautiful young woman sitting on a throne of gold. The woman was who we would later come to know as Elen of the Ways, though Macsen did not know her name at the time. He was immediately smitten, and the fair woman came toward him. Macsen took her in his arms and just as they were about to kiss, he was awoken by his men who suggested he eat something, as it was time to return to Rome.

Macsen's mood was gloomy, and he fell into a depression as a result of his inability to be with the fair maiden in his dream. He wouldn't eat or drink, and he neglected his duties until one day when his adviser confronted him, informing Macsen that his people were turning against him. He gathered his men and told them about the dream, explaining that he was in love with the woman he met in the dream and did not know if she was real or how to find her. It was decided that Macsen's men would set out throughout the land for a year and a day to try to find this woman.

Sadly, Macsen's men were not successful. Macsen was advised to return to the place where he had fallen asleep on the hunt in the hope that he might be able to remember the course of his dream journey that had led him to Elen. Macsen did so and was then able to give directions to his men that resulted in them finally finding the city of gold in Anglesey; the place Macsen had visited in his dream. When they saw Elen, the men fell to their knees and hailed her as the empress of Rome.

The men explained to Elen that Macsen had seen a vision of her in his dream and was now in love with her. They asked her to return to Rome with them, but Elen insisted that if Macsen truly loved her, he should come to her and ask her to marry him himself. Macsen journeyed to Anglesey, and when he arrived he saw the same vision that appeared to him in his dream. He threw his arms around Elen, proclaiming her to be his empress, and they were married that evening.

While we cannot say for sure that Elen sent the dream to Macsen, there are many clues to indicate that she used dream projection. Elen is based on a woman said to have lived in the fourth century, but she is also a sovereignty goddess. Sovereignty goddesses in the Celtic tradition typically have the ability and responsibility of bestowing sovereignty of the land upon the king. Without her doing so, the king would lose his power and the land would suffer, as each is a reflection of the other.

Many interpretations of this story point to Macsen's dream as an *aisling*, a dream known in Celtic tradition as one having a "strong spiritual message."[132] Elen's potential objective for sending such a dream makes sense, as further reading into the story shows their marriage unites Britain and Rome in more ways than one. Clues to Elen's gift with strategy are found in symbols in the story, such as the game board that Macsen sees in his dream and real-life encounter with her. Furthermore, as per custom at the time, a new bride may ask for a

---

132   Zteve T. Evans, "British Legends: Elen of the Hosts-Saint, Warrior Queen, Goddess of Sovereignty," Folklore Thursday website, June 1, 2018, https://folklorethursday .com/legends/british-legends-elen-of-the-hosts-saint-warrior-queen-goddess-of -sovereignty/.

wedding gift from her husband which he shall grant. Elen strategically asks that Britain and its islands be ruled by her and her father.

Associated with the migration of reindeer, Elen was the goddess of paths, trackways and ley lines, leading some to consider her the goddess of journeys, who made travel possible with her as a guide. It is therefore not unthinkable that she would have the power to project or send a dream to Macsen to get him to come to her.[133] In fact, many authors and scholars associate Elen with British shamanism as the goddess of dreams.[134]

While Elen's story might be one of the most detailed and well-known descriptions of dream projection, myths from a variety of cultures feature people being sent dreams. In Homer's *Iliad*, Zeus sent a dream to Agamemnon, commander of the Greek army, during the Trojan War. The Greek god Morpheus also had a reputation for sharing messages from the gods or prophetic information via dreams.

DEVELOPMENTS IN DREAM PROJECTION

Creating the content of someone else's dreams is not limited to deities. Many corporations and brands have been working on ways to influence our dreams for advertising purposes. According to a report in *Science*, cognitive scientist and PhD student at MIT Adam Haar has invented a glove that tracks sleep phases and provides audio cues to influence the wearer's dream content.[135] Haar says that Microsoft and at least two airlines have contacted him about his inventions, and researchers from renowned educational institutes are also acting

133   Evans, "British Legends," https://folklorethursday.com/legends/british-legends
      -elen-of-the-hosts-saint-warrior-queen-goddess-of-sovereignty/.
134   Judith Shaw, "Elen of the Ways," Feminism and Religion website, September 28, 2016,
      https://feminismandreligion.com/2016/09/28/elen-of-the-ways-by-judith-shaw/.
135   Moutinho, "Are advertisers coming for your dreams?" https://www.science.org
      /content/article/are-advertisers-coming-your-dreams/ *Science* website, June 11, 2021.

as consultants to help corporations conduct studies to gather information that could be used to influence our dreams.[136]

DREAM WALKING

Dream walking is somewhat different from dream projection though both cases involve infiltrating someone's dreams. Dream walking is typically defined as entering someone else's dreams, though the definition could also include pulling someone else into *your* dreams. In some cases, both you and the other person dream walk into a neutral space, all done through astral projection.

Dream walking can happen unintentionally. I have personally had dream walking experiences multiple times. In most cases, it occurred with someone that I was deeply connected to but who was no longer in my life. I lost contact with my first love for almost thirty years but throughout that time would have dreams at least once or twice a year where this person and I would simply hang out and talk. For a long time, I shrugged these dreams off as irrelevant creations of my subconscious. But when we reconnected, I found that many of the things he told me during these dreams actually occurred in his life.

Another loved one I lost contact with for some time appeared in my dreams pretty regularly over the years and would show me significant events in his life, such as marrying a woman with brown hair and brown eyes whom he told me in the dream was named after a plant. When we finally reconnected many years later, I learned that the woman he had married was named Heather and that she looked exactly as I described. Individuals I care about have come to me in dreams to let me know about a challenge they were facing. In all these cases, my intuition told me that something was amiss with these loved ones, but they were not willing or able to tell me what they

---

136   Moutinho, "Are advertisers coming for your dreams?" *Science* website, June 11, 2021.

were going through. It seems as though a part of them—perhaps their higher selves—felt the need to reach out in the dream world.

In one rather awkward dream encounter, I found myself sitting in a room with my ex-husband. Neither one of us seemed to know why we were there, especially since we weren't really communicating during our waking reality and had been having some conflicts. There was no hate between us, but there was definitely mistrust and a lack of understanding. The dream was helpful in that it seemed to allow us to clear the air a bit, though my ex-husband made it clear that he felt we shouldn't share dream space for the foreseeable future. I agreed, and we did not find ourselves meeting in our dreams again after that. The one thing that all these dreams had in common was that much like in my prophetic and underworld dreams, they had a different feel from my "normal" dreams.

ETHICS OF DREAM WALKING AND DREAM PROJECTION

Before I share information and techniques that can help with dream projection and dream walking, it is critical to cover ethics related to these specific types of dream magick. I am a strong advocate for ethical consideration when it comes to intentionally interfering with others' dreams, in part because I would not be comfortable with someone else infiltrating my dreams without my full knowledge and permission. In my opinion, being honest with the recipient of your dream magick and ensuring that they are okay with what you intend to do is not only respectful of their free will and less likely to do harm, it also increases the efficacy of your magick and can validate your efforts. Keep in mind that if you are having strong negative feelings about another person, it can unintentionally trigger dream walking or dream projection that can prove toxic for both you and the other person. The best way to avoid unintentional dream visitation is to be aware of your feelings and to work things out in your waking life or, if that is not feasible, redirect your thoughts to something positive that you wish to dream about. Meditation can also facilitate a more peaceful state of mind prior to sleep.

What about times when you aren't able to explicitly ask for permission, such as with someone in a coma or who is otherwise unable to communicate with you while awake? In these instances, I typically perform my dream magick with the stated caveat that my dream projection or dream walking only works if it does no harm to the recipient and if they are receptive. To be honest, dream magick is less likely to work as it is if the other person is not open to it. Some paths and individuals purposefully use dream magick with the intent to create mental discomfort or harm (e.g., as part of a hex or curse). While I do not personally feel comfortable using dream magick for this purpose, it is understandable that some would. However, those sorts of uses are not covered in this book.

METHODS FOR DREAM WALKING

Dream walking may seem like an impossible feat but that's simply not true. While it does take a great deal of patience, trial and error, and practice (perhaps even more so than other forms of dream magick), it is by no means impossible. As covered in chapter 6, many people have confessed to having a deceased loved one visit them in their dreams. If our loved ones can manage to cross out of the spirit world and into our dreams, surely we must be able to communicate through dreams with individuals who share this physical plane with us!

According to surveys, between 8 and 20 percent of people polled said that they had at least one out-of-body experience in their lifetime.[137] Some of these experiences happened organically as opposed

---

137 Callum McKelvie and Benjamin Radford, "Astral Projection: Facts and Theories," Live Science website, February 25, 2022, https://www.livescience.com/27978 -astral-projection.html.

to happening with intent. History shows us that belief in the possibility of astral projection has existed across many cultures and times. Theosophy, founded in the late 1800s by Helena Blavatsky, taught that one of the seven bodies that each human consisted of was an astral body that could leave the physical plane and travel to astral realms.[138] Science has not been able to definitively prove that astral projection exists, but some studies do point to the strong possibility that out-of-body experiences may be real. A 2014 study found that the cerebellum of a woman allegedly experiencing astral projection showed activation that was consistent with the experience the woman described while in her astral body.[139] The possibility of astral projection being real was substantial enough that, according to a now declassified document, the Central Intelligence Agency of the United States began doing research into astral projection in 1983.[140]

In addition to astral projection, lucid dreaming can be used for dream walking, but sustaining lucidity long enough to find the intended recipient and interact with them takes a great deal of effort and experience. Since lucid dreaming has already been covered, we'll focus on achieving astral projection as a foundation for meeting with others while dreaming. In my experience, astral projection has some features that don't regularly occur with lucid dreaming. Because astral projection has the potential to leave the physical body in a vulnerable state, I strongly suggest attempting this in a place where you are sure you won't be interrupted and that you cast a circle and ward as you normally would.

138   McKelvie and Radford, "Astral Projection: Facts and Theories," Live Science website, February 25, 2022.

139   Andra M. Smith and Claude Messier, "Voluntary Out-of-Body Experience: An fMRI study," *Frontiers in Human Neuroscience* 8, no. 70 (2014): https://www.frontiersin.org /articles/10.3389/fnhum.2014.00070/full.

140   "The CIA's Gateway Report on Astral Projection + Templeton's Consciousness Competition", Mind Science website, April 13, 2021, https://mindscience.org /neuro-news/the-cias-gateway-report-on-astral-projection-templetons-consciousness -competition/.

Astral projection involves intentionally separating the spirit or astral body from the physical body. While this can occur involuntarily in extreme circumstances such as when we are scared or feel unsafe, the best way to intentionally induce astral travel is to lay in a comfortable space and work on relaxing the body and mind. It's key to have a clear objective for your travel in your mind as you relax. Once you have achieved a state of relaxation, see in your mind's eye that your astral body is beginning to move out of and above your physical body.

The actual "loosening" of the spirit body is a unique experience, though many report that as their spirit body rises, it turns over, allowing them to see their physical body laying below. Don't be discouraged if this does not happen for you—I rarely see myself when I have an out-of-body experience; rather, my spirit body feels as though it is rocking back and forth, like being gently moved by ocean waves. Imagining each part of your spiritual body slowly disconnecting from your physical body (similar to a visualized body scan) is an effective way of focusing on the separation. I have also found that keeping crystals on or near my body and setting the tone in my environment with incense and soft music or shamanic drumming enhances my ability to trigger an out-of-body experience.

One thing that most people seem to agree about astral projection is the need to securely connect the physical body with the spirit body, often done by imagining a silver cord connecting the two bodies. A variation on this method is to imagine a cord extending from your body up into the sky and climbing the cord into the astral realm with your spirit body. From there, the cord is envisioned as tied to the spirit body to maintain connection with the physical body.

It is critical that you become familiar with and capable of having out-of-body experiences during your waking hours if at all possible. The more frequently you have these experiences while awake—even if only for a few minutes several times a week—the more likely it is that you can purposefully astrally project your dream self into another person's dream. As you become more proficient in astral projection, you'll want to begin initiating astral projection right before you fall asleep. Be sure to hold your desired destination in mind as you drift off to sleep in a semi- or fully astral state.

Another method for dream walking as described by author Debra Taitel takes a bit of a different approach. Meditate and set the stage for full relaxation as described in the instructions above. However, instead of setting a destination for your dream, you establish an intent to walk next to yourself in your dreams as if you were your own invisible twin.[141] Set the intent to be aware of everything you see in your dream and remember these details upon waking. In the first stages of practicing, you will simply be an observer rather than initiate activity or discussion in your dreams. After you have performed this method enough that you can consistently observe and recall your sleep journeys, you can begin to adapt the practice to travel to a specific person or place and initiate activity.

Dream Walking and Dream Projection Exercises

In this section are two activities to help you achieve dream projection and dream walking. Again, you are much more likely to achieve your goals if the dreamer you are targeting is aware of your intent and is willing. Success is a great deal more likely with this type of dream magick when working with someone you know. The added

---

141   Debra Taitel, "How to Effortlessly Dream Walk," Medium website March 18, 2022, https://debrataitel.medium.com/how-to-effortlessly-dream-walk-cfbafe1cae34.

benefit of working with someone who is aware and willing is that you can validate your experiences and learn what works for you and what doesn't.

For successful objective validation in dream projection, it's best to refrain from sharing details about the contents of the dream with your collaborator; instead, state that you will be sending them a dream. As for dream walking, I find it's best (at least at first) to not have a defined meeting place; a neutral space is often the most ideal location for interacting with another person while dreaming. The exception is if there is a special place in the waking world that has great emotional meaning or attachment for both dreamers, in which case it may be an easier location to access.

Dream Projection Poppet
Instructions

1. Begin by making a dream doll using the instructions in chapter 3. However, instead of making the poppet to be aligned with a deity, it will represent the person you wish to send a dream to. While the poppet doesn't have to explicitly resemble the person, customize it so that it aligns with the other person's energy. For example, you might use colors or patterns that this person likes. If you have personal items such as a strand of their hair, include it in the stuffing for the poppet. Other additions to the stuffing may include a picture (or a copy) of the person, their name or nickname written on a piece of paper, or a particular herb or scent that the person uses or is drawn to.

2. When you have finished creating the poppet, sew another flap of fabric to the back of the doll to make a pocket large enough to hold a small piece of paper.

3. On a small piece of paper, make a collage or drawing symbolic and descriptive of the dream you intend to send. You could describe the dream using words as a last resort, but remember that the language of our subconscious is generally symbolic and visual; written words are not as likely to be effective.

4. Place the paper in the pocket attached to the doll. During the day, place the doll on your dream altar. At night, place the doll under your pillow or near your bed.

5. Alternate placing the dream doll on your altar during the day and under your pillow or near your bed during the evening for three consecutive days and nights. Each night, before you go to sleep, state your intention clearly by naming the recipient of this dream and stating that this person will receive your dream within one week. Visualize the content of the dream as you drift off to sleep.

As always, record the results in your dream journal, especially if you are in communication with the dream recipient. If the dream does not happen right away, do not give up! Dream projection is an advanced magickal practice that takes time to master.

If the dream recipient is someone who learns best by sound or is very immersed in music, there's a wonderful technique you can incorporate into dream projection to boost the power of your intent. Talk with your intended dream recipient (if you are in contact) and find a song that they really enjoy or that has significance for them. Let them know that this song will be their "cue" to allow the dream projection to reach them. Listen to this song repeatedly as you make the poppet and the visual image placed in its pocket. Listen to the song again on the three nights that you attempt to project your dream. Ask your recipient to create a playlist with this song somewhere in the middle or toward the end and have them listen to the playlist each night as they fall asleep. Our subconscious mind hears and processes every bit of sound input that happens both when we are awake and sleep. When the selected song plays, it will act as a cue for their subconscious to be open and ready to receive your dream.

Dream Walking Amulet
Materials

+ A small cloth or felt bag
+ Something to represent you: a favorite item, a picture, song lyrics that you resonate with, or a piece of jewelry that has great meaning for you
+ Something to represent the person you wish to connect with; it should correspond with their essence and resonates with their energy
+ 2 small pieces of gold yarn or cord
+ A pinch of mugwort
+ A pinch of African dream root powder or a small piece of the root itself
+ A pinch of lemongrass
+ 2 rose petals (yellow or white for friendship, pink or red if the recipient is your significant other)
+ A pinch of lavender
+ A blue chime candle

Instructions

1. Hold the bag open and state the name of the other person that you wish to interact with while sleeping and state clearly your intent to dream walk to this person once you

fall asleep. This bag will act as a connector, similar to the phone number of a person you wish to call.

2. Place your items in the bag, followed by the items to represent the other person. Tie two of the items together using one of the gold cords.

3. As you place the mugwort in the bag, state, "I add this mugwort to strengthen the lines of psychic communication."

4. As you place the African dream root in the bag, state, "I add African dream root for powerful dream magick."

5. As you place the lemongrass in the bag, state, "I call on lemongrass to open the way."

6. Add the pinch of lavender for relaxation and maintaining connections.

7. Add the rose petals as a symbol of your friendship or love.

8. Once you have placed everything in the bag, hold it in your hands while visualizing your intent. If you still have a piece of gold yarn or cord available, use this to tie the bag closed.

9. Place the bag on your dream altar and light the blue chime candle to represent strong communication and connection. As the candle burns down, form a clear visual image in your mind of the person you wish to meet in your dream journeys and imagine an energetic gold cord extending from your heart chakra to theirs. Next, imagine the two of you facing each other and dark purple energy emerging from both of your third eye chakras, mingling together in the space between the two of you.

10. When the candle burns down, remove the bag from the altar and either put it under your pillow or near your bed. As you drift off to sleep, hold your intention to dream walk

in your mind and visualize the person you wish to visit in your dreams. Just like dream projection, dream walking is an advanced form of magick, so it may take time to see the results you are hoping for. The more you practice your dream walking attempts, the more likely you will eventually be successful in your efforts.

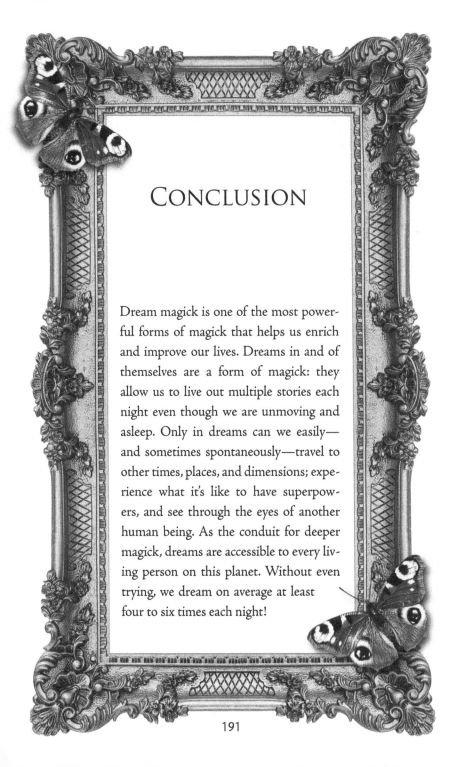

CONCLUSION

Dream magick is one of the most powerful forms of magick that helps us enrich and improve our lives. Dreams in and of themselves are a form of magick: they allow us to live out multiple stories each night even though we are unmoving and asleep. Only in dreams can we easily—and sometimes spontaneously—travel to other times, places, and dimensions; experience what it's like to have superpowers, and see through the eyes of another human being. As the conduit for deeper magick, dreams are accessible to every living person on this planet. Without even trying, we dream on average at least four to six times each night!

Perhaps the reason I am so passionate about dream magick is that I have seen the transformative power of dreams play out in so many areas of my life and the lives of others. There are few other forms of magick that have the ability to help us gain such a deep understanding of ourselves and our needs in a way that not only allows us to unleash our potential but also helps us gain confidence and love ourselves more. I have been able to travel to exotic places and have adventures that would have been out of reach in my waking life. Within dreams, physical and mental healing are as possible as connecting with loved ones both living and dead. I cannot think of another form of magick that achieves all of these things and more—sometimes all in the same night!

As you have read, dream magick is by no means easy: It takes a great deal of patience, resilience, receptivity, and intentional effort. It also requires practice, but fortunately we have the opportunity to practice every time we close our eyes. Despite the sustained effort and fortitude necessary for success, the rewards you can expect from doing this type of magick far outweigh the challenges, in my opinion. As unreachable as your goals may sometimes seem, remember that there are no limitations in a dream. It is my hope that by reading this book you too will have the tools you need to achieve your dream goals and by doing so manifest greater happiness, health, creativity, understanding, and self-love. May you have the sweetest of dreams!

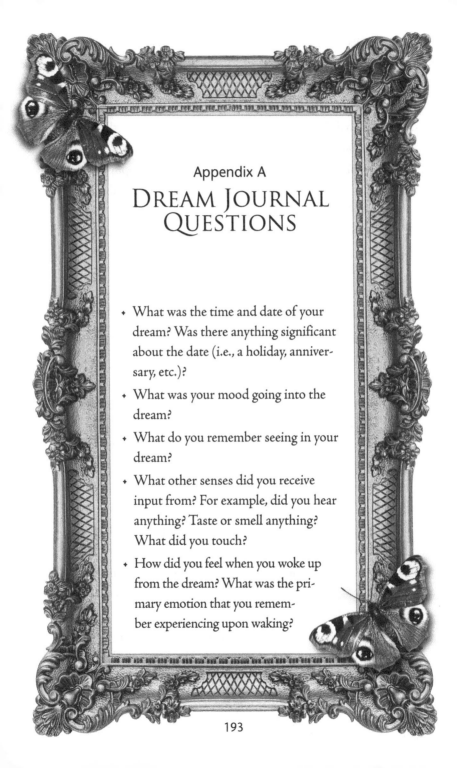

Appendix A
DREAM JOURNAL QUESTIONS

+ What was the time and date of your dream? Was there anything significant about the date (i.e., a holiday, anniversary, etc.)?

+ What was your mood going into the dream?

+ What do you remember seeing in your dream?

+ What other senses did you receive input from? For example, did you hear anything? Taste or smell anything? What did you touch?

+ How did you feel when you woke up from the dream? What was the primary emotion that you remember experiencing upon waking?

+ Was there anything in your dream that related to the day's or week's events? How did those play out in your dreams?

+ Who did you see in your dreams? Do you know these people in your waking life?

+ If you saw people in your dreams, were they represented as they are when you normally interact with them? If not, what was different about them?

+ Was there anything unusual about your dream? Were you able to do things that you normally couldn't such as fly or put your hand through a wall?

+ Do you recall any lucidity? If so, what occurred? Were you an observer or did you influence the content of the dream?

+ Were there any visitations from deceased loved ones or other individuals?

+ How many hours of sleep did you get?

+ Were any of your dreams repetitive dreams that you've had before? If so, what message do you think this dream is trying to convey? Are there common triggers or life events that have occurred repeatedly when you have had these dreams?

+ Were there any symbols that stood out to you? If so, consult your dream dictionary to try and interpret them.

+ Where did your dream take place? What time of day did it occur?

+ What was the moon phase the night of your dream? What were the astrological conditions (i.e., Moon in a particular house, blue moon, eclipse, etc.)?

+ Did you attempt any dream magick prior to your dream? If so, were you able to accomplish your objective? What worked? What didn't?

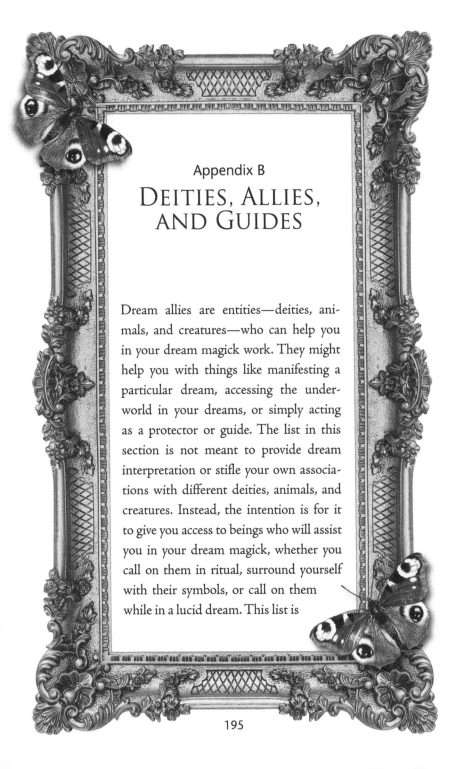

Appendix B
DEITIES, ALLIES, AND GUIDES

Dream allies are entities—deities, animals, and creatures—who can help you in your dream magick work. They might help you with things like manifesting a particular dream, accessing the underworld in your dreams, or simply acting as a protector or guide. The list in this section is not meant to provide dream interpretation or stifle your own associations with different deities, animals, and creatures. Instead, the intention is for it to give you access to beings who will assist you in your dream magick, whether you call on them in ritual, surround yourself with their symbols, or call on them while in a lucid dream. This list is not exhaustive; it is intended to give you a diverse starting point in looking for dream allies.

Deities

Anubis (Egyptian): Jackal headed god of funerary rites and guide to the underworld.

Arianrhod (Welsh): Goddess of the silver wheel who is said to reside in the sky. She appears in *The Mabinogion.*

Asklepios (Greek): Also known as Asclepius, god of healing and medicine. He was the son of Apollo. There were many dream incubation temples dedicated to him throughout the Mediterranean and beyond.

Ayezan (Voodoo): Also goes by Ayzan and Ayizan. Papa Legba's wife, she is known for guarding boundaries and doorways and is very knowledgeable about the spirit realm.

Bes (Egyptian): Also known as Bisu and Aha, Bes has the appearance of a dwarf and is a notable warrior. Also presides over fertility, the home, entertainment, and sexuality.

Breksta (Lithuanian): Goddess of the night and dreams. Was said to protect humans from sunrise to sunset.[142]

Caer Ibormeith (Pan-Celtic): Worshipped in Ireland, Scotland, and Wales, Caer was the goddess of dreams and prophecy. She was a daughter of the Tuatha Dé Danaan and known to interchangeably take the form of a beautiful woman or a swan. She chose her true love, Aengus Og, by appearing to him in a dream.

---

142   Valda Roric, "Ancient Gods—When Dreams Ruled the World," Ancient Origins website, updated June 11, 2016, https://www.ancient-origins.net/myths-legends/ancient-gods-when-darkness-ruled-world-006067.

Ceridwen (Welsh): Also known as Cerridwen. Welsh goddess known for brewing a potion in her cauldron that would provide *Awen*, or "divine transformation." Shapeshifter.

Chang'E (Chinese): Also known as Chang'O, Chang'E is the goddess of the moon and associated with the hare. She is said to have stolen the drug of immortality from her lover, Hou Yi.[143]

Elen of the Ways (Welsh): Also known as Elen of the Hosts, a sovereignty goddess said to be based on a real person. Her story is included in *The Mabinogion*. She is known for sending a dream to the Roman emperor Macsen Wledig and for creating tracks and pathways. She is associated with reindeer.

Erzulie (Voodoo): Also known as Ezili. Presides over love, women, and bodies of water. She is a guide who can travel via water and can act as a mirror, reflecting back to us our deepest thoughts and secrets.

Hades (Greek): God of the underworld. His consort is Persephone, who is also the goddess of spring. Hades can help one to connect with deceased ancestors and loved ones.

Hermes (Greek): Known as both the trickster and the messenger in the Hellenic pantheon, Hermes is a psychopomp who brings the deceased to the underworld. He oversees communications and protects travelers.

Hypnos (Greek): God of sleep and father of Morpheus. He is the son of Nyx and the brother of Thanatos and is said to live in the underworld.

Ishtar (Akkadian/Assyrian): Sometimes identified as a form of the Sumerian goddess Inanna, Ishtar is the goddess of war

---

143   Matt Stefon, "Chang'e," Britannica website, last updated December 1, 2023, https://www.britannica.com/topic/Change-Chinese-deity.

and sexuality. She is said to have appeared before her king on occasion in dreams to let him know what was occurring in the world.

Mamu (Mesopotamian): Daughter of Utu, said to preside over the world of dreams.[144]

Manannán Mac Lir (Celtic): Irish god who presides over the ocean. He has a magical crane bag that holds treasures rendered invisible in an ebbing tide.

Morana (Slavic): Goddess of winter and death who lives in what was known as the "Mirror Place," believed to be the underworld.[145]

Morpheus (Greek): God who could shape the dreams of those who were asleep. Brother of the spirits known as oneiroi.

Morrigan (Celtic): Irish goddess of war sometimes viewed as a triplicity comprised of goddesses including Badb, Macha, and Nemain. Associated with crows, prophecy, and inciting battle frenzies in warriors.

Nephthys (Egyptian): Sister of Isis, Nephthys is the goddess of dreams and air.

Nótt (Norse): Mentioned in the Edda, Nótt is the Norse goddess of night, sleep and dreams. She has a dark appearance and rides a chariot given to her by the god Odin.[146]

Nuit (Egyptian): Mother of Isis, Osiris, Set, and Nepythys, Nuit is the goddess of the night sky. She is believed to stretch

---

144   James Hardy, "The 10 Most Important Sumerian Gods: Nammu, Enki, Enlil, and More!" History Cooperative website, April 22, 2022, https://historycooperative.org /sumerian-gods/.

145   Veronica Parkes, "A Cycle of Life and Death-Slavic Goddesses Morana and Vesna," Ancient Origins website, June 29, 2021, https://www.ancient-origins.net/myths -legends/morana-vesna-006984.

146   Molly Khan, "Nott, the Dream Goddess of Night and Darkness," Heathen at Heart (blog), last updated February 25, 2019, https://www.patheos.com/blogs /heathenatheart/2019/02/nott-the-dream-goddess/.

across the sky at the end of day and is often depicted as a
naked blue woman with stars on her body.

Papa Ghede (Voodoo): Also known as Papa Gede. Typically
dressed in stylish black tails, a top hat, and sunglasses, Papa
Ghede rules over the voodoo spirits of death and birth who
bear his name. Like many psychopomp deities, Papa Ghede
can help us to travel back and forth in the dream realm.

Papa Legba (Voodoo): Similar in some ways to Papa Ghede,
Papa Legba is the loa of the crossroads and doors. He is a
liaison between our world and the spirit world and is known
to remove obstacles. Papa Legba excels at communication
and conveying information.

Persephone (Greek): Consort of Hades, Persephone is both
the goddess of spring and the queen of the underworld, making her a ruler over birth and death. She is helpful in efforts
to contact the spirit realm.

Rhiannon (Celtic): Welsh sovereignty goddess said to have
three birds that could sing one to sleep and bring the dead
back to life. She is also said to be associated with Annwn, the
Celtic otherworld.

Vishnu (Hindu): In the Vedanta Sutra, the material world is
described as being a dream had by Vishnu. He is known as
the "All-Pervading One" and is able to defy time and space by
being in all places at once.

ANIMALS AND INSECTS

Bats: Bats are associated with darkness and night. This, combined with their ability to travel and their sensitivity to sound
make them good allies in helping us travel through the dream
realm, pay attention to details, and uncover what is hidden in
the dark.

Bees: Bees have a long history of being associated with the Divine and the ability to travel between realms. They are hard workers, and if you are able to convince them to assist you, they will be quite loyal.

Butterflies: Butterflies are symbols of transformation, and their wings allow them to travel easily. Just like humans who sleep at night, caterpillars must rest in a cocoon before they can transform. Work with a butterfly if you are trying to transform any aspect of your life or yourself.

Cats: Cats have been popular with witches for ages, probably due in part to their ability to pick up on things that we humans normally can't. They are incredibly sensitive to energy and were important enough in Egyptian history to be worshipped and treated with care. I have had more than one cat be an ally in my magickal workings and visit me in dreams. Work with a cat ally for general dream magick, to gain clarity, and to move swiftly through different realms in your dreams.

Crows and ravens: While both are in the genus Corvus, they are different birds. However, both have been associated with messages, prophecy, and the night probably due in part to their inky black appearance. Many consider them magical creatures, and they can make wonderful allies in dream projection and accessing prophetic dreams.

Deer: These gentle animals are associated with sensitivity and intuition. They can be quite graceful and still when they wish to be, which may be why I've found deer helpful as allies in both dream work and working with the spirit realm. In addition, stags are considered particularly lucky creatures in multiple traditions. Work with deer to access the underworld in dreams as well as to heighten your intuition.

Dogs: Faithful and loving, dogs have been favorite familiars of deities such as Hecate and Asklepios. Dogs can be great protectors and companions in dream work.

Dolphins: Playful and intelligent, dolphins can be amenable to working with humans. Their sense of playfulness can help you take a more relaxed approach if you find yourself getting impatient or frustrated with your dream magick efforts. Dolphins also have strong intuition.

Eagles: Birds in general make good dream allies, and eagles are often thought to be some of the most powerful. Because they can soar very high, they are sometimes thought of as messengers and links to the Divine. Eagles can aid greatly in dream projection and travels to different dream realms. They can also help you gain clarity in understanding your dreams.

Frogs: Frogs have long been associated with magick. In addition to being associated with weather magick, they are also associated with fertility and forward movement due to their growth progression from a tadpole into a frog. Work with frog when you are trying to do dreamwork to predict the weather or to do dream incubation to stimulate fertility and creativity.

Hawks: Another strong dream ally, as they are believed to be visionaries who can grant the power of foresight. Work with hawks to manifest prophetic and problem-solving dreams.

Homing Pigeon: It may seem like an odd entry, but hear me out. In the midst of writing this appendix, my husband quietly called for me to come out to our deck. There, sitting on the railing, was a beautiful white and gray pigeon with purplish-green iridescent feathers around its neck and a tag on one of its feet. After singing, cooing and gently talking to it, the pigeon came near me and seemed to be listening closely for a while before flying away. Homing pigeons have a history as messengers and are very intelligent. They are also able to consistently find their way back home after being sent away. Working with the humble homing pigeon can be very beneficial when you are trying to navigate the dream world or send messages to others via dreams.

Horses: Horses have been the allies of many deities, including the Welsh goddess Rhiannon and the Greek god Poseidon. They are revered for their strength, stamina, and swiftness. Work with horses as allies when traveling between realms as part of your dream magick.

Owls: Owls are nocturnal birds that represent wisdom, strength, insight, intuition, and prophecy. They also sometimes act as travelers to and from the spirit realm. Owls see in three dimensions and have excellent night vision, both of which qualities lend them to astral projection. They can spot prey from far above, even in snow. Work with owls when you are trying to see a situation from many different angles in your dream, when you wish to have a prophetic dream, and when you wish to travel between realms.

Snakes: Symbols of transformation and kundalini energy, snakes are associated with deities such as Asklepios and Hermes. Snakes move fast and are able to slither in and out of places that can be difficult to access. They can be great allies in dream travel and also act as protectors in dreamwork.

Spiders: Spiders weave their webs just as our subconscious weaves our dreams. Call upon spiders for help with dream incubation.

Wolves: Wolves are very protective of their packs and are superior pathfinders—both qualities that align with dream magick. Work with wolves when you need to find multiple possible solutions for a problem, find someone in your dreams, or if you desire protection in your dream magick efforts.

MYTHOLOGICAL CREATURES AND OTHER ALLIES

Dragons: Revered by the Chinese, dragons are powerful and protective of what they consider theirs. They have the gift of prophecy and the ability to travel great distances by air and, in some cases, water. Dragons can be of great assistance when you need protection, insight, or wish to travel in your dream magick efforts.

Medusa: You might be wondering what good Medusa can possibly do for you in dream magick, but I have worked with her in this capacity many times with great success. While she doesn't assist with accessing dreams, once you are in one, she can help you to journey to places that may seem dangerous. If Medusa is willing to work with you, she doesn't hesitate to go ahead of you when making your way into locations that may be unsafe. If anything hostile attempts to harm you, Medusa can stop them with a stare, not only helping you avoid harm but also giving you the opportunity to safely examine hostile images, as they could be messengers from your subconscious. Medusa is also able to act as a mirror, reflecting those parts of your subconscious that you may need to see.

Mermaids: Mermaids can act as allies by taking you into the depths of your subconscious via dreams. Intuition, empathy, shapeshifting, and telepathy are all magical abilities that mermaids possess and can help you to attain.

Menshen: The Chinese guardians of doors and rooms who protected those sleeping within, their images are often

painted on doors to temples China.[147] Work with the Menshen in accessing unfamiliar places in your dreams or places
that you are having a difficult time getting in to.

Oneiroi: Under the leadership of Morpheus, these dream
spirits would emerge at night in the form of bats. They had
the ability to bring both dreams of prophecy and nightmares.
Work with the oneiroi to manifest prophetic dreams and to
understand your nightmares.

Pegasus: The legendary son of Medusa, Pegasus has all the
powers of the horse and the extra bonus of wings. Pegasus
was reputed to be able to pass between the worlds of the
mortals and immortals and therefore can be an ally when you
are attempting to access other realms in your dreams such as
the Underworld.

Phoenix: As the legend goes, the Phoenix is a beautiful, fiery
bird that regenerates over various cycles. Each time the
Phoenix dies, it is reborn again from its own ashes. The
Phoenix provides strength and is a symbol of transformation
and rebirth. Phoenix as an ally can help you to go wherever it
is you wish to go in your dreams and can help you transform
your dreams while in a lucid state.

---

147   Emily Mark, "Most Popular Gods and Goddesses of Ancient China," World History
website, updated April 25, 2016, https://www.worldhistory.org/article/894/most
-popular-gods--goddesses-of-ancient-china/.

Appendix C

Herbal, Crystal, Oil, and Astrological Correspondences

Astrological

Correspondences such as moon phases and astrological occurrences can have an impact on dream experiences and dream magick efforts. Here are some common correspondences to consider when doing dreamwork.

> **Waxing moon:** Tends to help with building momentum for efforts such as dream manifestation and projection
>
> **Full moon:** The moon has the most effect on our emotions in this phase, but some find it disruptive to their sleep patterns. When the moon is full,

it is at its most powerful, making it advantageous for dream work that requires charging anything with energy, dream manifestation, and dream projection.

Waning moon: Good for many dream healing efforts, contacts with the deceased, and shadow work via dreams.

Eclipses: Both lunar and solar eclipses are conducive times for charging water, crystals, and amulets for dream work. Eclipses can represent beginnings and endings and are a good time for starting over or clearing something from the past. Dream work done during an eclipse can be more intense than usual.

Blue moon: This is a very powerful time to do dream work, especially any involving glamour magick, such as enhancing or changing your appearance in a dream or for weaving a dream.

Mercury in retrograde: This is not a time that works well for most forms of dream magick, especially dreams involving any kind of communication or travel. Sleep may be disrupted when Mercury is in retrograde, and you may have more stress-related dreams.

Ninth house: The ninth house in your natal chart is represented by Sagittarius and the planet Jupiter, and it is the house most related to our dreams. The zodiac sign in your ninth house will determine how it manifests in your life. [148]

Although beyond the scope of this book, learning more about astrological phases and each house in your chart can enrich dream work as well.

---

148   Sarah Regan, "Everything You Need to Know About the 9th House and What It Means In Your Birth Chart," MBG Mindfulness website, December 20, 2022, https:// www.mindbodygreen.com/articles/ninth-house-in-astrology#:~:text=The%20ninth %20house%20is%20connected,religion%2C%20morals%2C%20and%20ethics.

Herbs

I created the following list of herbs and oils based on my herbalism studies and experience. Herbs and oils can be used in a variety of ways including in oil diffusers, dream dolls, bath teas, dream pillows, topical application (for oils), incense, and teas or tisanes for consumption. If you plan on ingesting or applying any of these herbs, start with very small doses until you have a better sense of how your body reacts with the herb. Any essential oil should be diluted in a carrier oil such as almond or grapeseed if you are planning on applying it topically.

> **Note:** Please research herbs and oils before using them. Some herbs and oils are not safe during pregnancy or may have side effects or contraindications with other health conditions or prescription medications.

> **African dream root:** Can cause vivid or lucid dreams. The Xhosa people of South Africa also used it to communicate with ancestors in their dreams.[149]

> **Blue lotus flower:** Associated with the Egyptian Sun God, Ra. A sedative, it is mentioned in the Egyptian Book of the Dead and has a long history of use in dream magick.

> **Frankincense (resin):** Good for awakening consciousness and lucid dreaming. Connected with the Welsh goddess Arianrhod as well as with Egyptian embalming rites.

> **Jasmine:** Aids with restful sleep and prophetic dreams.

> **Lavender:** A very relaxing herb that can help you to relax and settle your mind prior to doing dream work.

---

149 Ryan Raman, "African Dream Root: Compounds, Effects, Downsides, and More," Healthline website, April 15, 2021, https://www.healthline.com/nutrition/suma-root-benefits-downsides.

Lemongrass: Aids with opening awareness, purification, and heightening psychic ability.

Lemon balm: Good for relaxation and dream recall.

Mugwort: One of the most popular dream allies. Helps with dream recall, prophetic dreams, vividness, and lucidity.

Myrrh (resin): Used for purification and protection and as incense for funerary rites.

Peppermint: Increases vividness of dreams.

Rose: Rose petals have a calming energy and can be used for emotional support for dream work. Roses also have the highest frequency of any plant, making them a wonderful ally in dream walking and projection.

Rosemary: Good for dream recall.

Sandalwood: Helps with relaxation.

Spearmint: Aids with prophetic dreams and communication. Enhances mental powers and assists with travel.

Valerian root: Helps with relaxation and sleep.

Vervain: Good for prophetic dreams.

Yarrow: Good for inducing dreams, especially prophetic dreams.

OILS

Anise seed: Known for preventing nightmares.

Blue lotus flower

Clary sage: Helps facilitate deep relaxation and gives deep insight via dreams.

Frankincense

Geranium: Stimulates psychic activity and is a good ally for dream work, especially astral projection. Also good for enhancing creativity.

Helichrysum: Works well for treating insomnia.

Jasmine

Lavender

Lemongrass

Patchouli: Good for anxiety that prevents sleep. Reputed to draw others to you and therefore could be used in dream walking.

Peppermint

Rose

Rosemary

Sandalwood

CRYSTALS, GEMS, AND ROCKS

Crystals can be used in dream dolls or pillows, as a talisman or in amulets, in crystal grids, placed on chakras or under your pillow, and in crystal water essences, though please note that some crystals, such as malachite, become toxic when placed in water or other liquids and should not be ingested. Other crystals below a level 6 on the Mohs scale of hardness have a tendency to dissolve or sustain damage when placed in water. These include but are not limited to selenite, opals, and calcite. Do your research prior to immersing crystals in water for purposes of ingestion or cleansing. Also, be sure to handle your crystals carefully; some are fragile.

Azurite: Helpful for seeking wisdom in dreams.

Amethyst: Good for intuition, dream recall, lucid dreaming, and dream manifestation.

Angel aura quartz: Help with accessing other realms, such as the dream realm. Promotes lucid, vivid dreams.

Blue kyanite: Is known to have a high vibration. Good for purification, communication, and seeking truth.

Celestite: Relaxing crystal that can help decode dream symbols and messages that appear to be coming from an ancestor or higher power.

Clear quartz: Clear Quartz is a good all-purpose dream magick crystal, as it can be programmed for specific dream work, e.g., lucid dreaming. It also helps with problem-solving and clarity.

Citrine: Citrine is one of very few crystals able to transform negative energies without needing to be regularly cleansed. This crystal can be helpful in overcoming nightmares as well as efforts to increase the number of dreams and their recall.

Herkimer diamond: A powerful third eye chakra stone that also acts as an ally in dream recall.

Labradorite: Good for underworld dreaming due to its reputed connection to the spirit world.

Lapis lazuli: Helps to induce clairvoyance in dreams.

Lepidolite: Helps with insomnia, anxiety, protection, and easing bad dreams.

Malachite: Malachite is a stone with many uses. It offers protection and transformation, absorbs negative energies, and has the ability to stimulate dreams. However, malachite also tends to reveal truths we might not want to see. Malachite can provide clarity and can overcome fear while strengthening willpower. Malachite can be toxic, so do not drink any water with malachite in it, and stay away from powdered malachite—accidentally inhaling it can be harmful to your health.

Merlinite: Draws out toxins and negative energy. Can provide powerful healing and gentle energy for those experiencing nightmares and other traumas.

Moldavite: While moldavite is a very powerful ally, it can be too much for some people. Technically not a crystal, moldavite is formed when a meteorite hits the earth. However, we can use it in the same way we use other gemstones. Moldavite is stimulating and aids in lucid dreaming, dream projection or dream walking, and connecting to spirits. Be aware that it can very quickly bring about change and truths you might not want to see.

Moonstone: Moonstone enhances intuition and can help relax nervous minds.

Obsidian: Obsidian is used for protection and connecting with spirits. Can be too grounding/heavy for some, so you may want to balance it out with a higher energy crystal such as quartz or blue kyanite.

Rose quartz: The energy of rose quartz is one of love and compassion. It is a calming stone that can release emotional blockages. Rose quartz also helps to assuage grief, which can be beneficial when you've had a visitation from a deceased loved one.

White howlite: White howlite can be a very relaxing stone that helps with memory, making it a good crystal for dream recall. It can also improve communication and facilitate patience.

BIBLIOGRAPHY

Abrams, Zara. "Growing Concerns About Sleep." *American Psychological Association* 40, no. 4 (2021). https://www.apa.org/monitor/2021/06/news-concerns-sleep.

Acher, Frater. "A Course in Dream Magic Part I." Theo Magica website (n.d.). https://theomagica.com/dream-magic-part-1.

Allrich, Karri Ann. *A Witch's Book of Dreams: Understanding the Power of Dreams and Symbols.* St. Paul, MN: Llewellyn Publishing, 2001.

American Botanical Council. "Blue Lotus—Lily of the Sun." ABC

Herbalgram website, December 15, 2020. https://www
.herbalgram.org/resources/herbclip/herbclip-news/2020
/bluelotus/.

Anuradha. "Vishnu Sustains the Universe." All About Hinduism
website, March 8, 2013. https://www.allabouthinduism
.info/2013/03/08/vishnu-the-protector/.

Asals, Katharine. "Chapter 2: Dream Theory in Native North
America." Katharine Asals website, (n.d.). https://
katharineasals.com/articles/the-trope-of-the-dream-and
-other-irrational-moments/chapter-2-dream-theory
-in-native-north-america/.

Baird, Christopher S. "Do Blind People Dream in Visual Images?"
Science Questions with Surprising Answers website, February
11, 2020. https://www.wtamu.edu/~cbaird/sq/2020/02/11
/do-blind-people-dream-in-visual-images/.

Barnes, Celeste. "Apollo" in *Naming the God*. Edited by Trevor
Greenfield. Winchester, UK: Moon Books, 2022.

Belanger, Michelle. *Psychic Dreamwalking: Explorations at the
Edge of Self*. San Francisco: Red Wheel/Weiser, 2006.

Boyer, Corinne. *Dream Divination Plants in the Northern European
Tradition*. Hercules, CA: Three Hands Press, 2022.

Brown, Nimue. *Pagan Dreaming: The Magic of Altered
Consciousness*. Winchester, UK: Moon Books, 2015.

Burkert, Walter. *Greek Religion: Archaic and Classical*. Cambridge,
MA: Harvard University Press, 1987.

Callaway, Ewen. "Fearful Memories Passed Down to Mouse
Descendants." *Scientific American* website. December 1, 2013.
https://www.scientificamerican.com/article/fearful
-memories-passed-down/. Originally published in *Nature*
magazine.

Carey Jr., Harold. "Owl and Woodpecker—A Navajo Tale." Navajo People website. January 9, 2015. https://navajopeople.org/blog /owl-and-woodpecker-a-navajo-tale/.

Carr, M., R. Borcsok, M. Taylor et al. "0159 Reduced REM Sleep Percent in Frequent Cannabis vs. Non-Cannabis Users." *Sleep* 43, supplement 1 (2020): A62–A63. https://academic.oup.com /sleep/article/43/Supplement_1/A62/5846891.

Casale, Alessandro. "Indigenous Dreams: Prophetic Nature, Spirituality, and Survivance." Indigenous New Hampshire Collaborative Collective website (n.d.). https://indigenousnh .com/2019/01/25/indigenous-dreams/.

Chatland, Jan. "Descriptions of Various Loa of Voodoo," Webster University website. 1990. http://faculty.webster.edu/corbetre /haiti/voodoo/biglist.htm.

Centers for Disease Control and Prevention. "Circadian Rhythms and Circadian Clock." Updated April 1, 2020. https://archive. cdc.gov/#/details?url=https://www.cdc.gov/niosh/emres /longhourstraining/clock.html.

Den Hollander, Juliette. "History of Dream Research," Sutori website (n.d.). https://www.sutori.com/en/story/the -history-of-dream-research-aHZ2EkuAQtRJgjhMMjxJ7bvX.

Dispenza, Joe. *Evolve Your Brain: The Science of Changing Your Mind.* Deerfield Beach, FL: Health Communications, 2007.

Evans, Zteve T. "British Legends: Elen of the Hosts-Saint, Warrior Queen, Goddess of Sovereignty." Folklore Thursday website. June 1, 2018. https://folklorethursday.com/legends/british -legends-elen-of-the-hosts-saint-warrior-queen-goddess-of -sovereignty/.

Fritscher, Lisa. "Carl Jung's Collective Unconscious Theory: What It Suggests About the Mind." VeryWellMind website. May 17,

2023. https://www.verywellmind.com/what-is-the-collective
-unconscious-2671571.

Garfield, Patricia. *Creative Dreaming: Plan and Control Your Dreams
to Develop Creativity, Overcome Fears, Solve Problems, and Create
a Better Self.* New York: Simon and Schuster, 1995.

Glenn, Gigi. "Ghede: Voodoo Spirits in New Orleans Traditions,"
ViaNolaVie website. November 2, 2020, https://
www.vianolavie.org/2020/11/02/ghede-voodoo-spirits
-in-new-orleans-traditions/.

Gregoire, Carolyn. "8 Famous Ideas That Came From Dreams (Literally)," *Huff Post* website. November 16, 2013. https://www
.huffpost.com/entry/famous-ideas-from-dreams_n_4276838.

Hardy, James. "The 10 Most Important Sumerian Gods: Nammu,
Enki, Enlil and More!" History Cooperative website. April 22,
2022, https://historycooperative.org/sumerian-gods/.

Hennessy, William. "The Ancient Irish Goddess of War." Sacred
Texts website. https://sacred-texts.com/neu/celt/aigw/aigw01
.htm. Originally published 1870.

Henriques, Martha. "Can the legacy of trauma be passed down the
generations?" *BBC* website. March 26, 2019, https://www.bbc
.com/future/article/20190326-what-is-epigenetics.

Hill, J., "Bes." Ancient Egypt Online website. 2010.
https://ancientegyptonline.co.uk/bes/.

"History of Dream Interpretation." Oniri website. August
10, 2022, https://www.oniri.io/post/a-bit-of-history-of
-dream-interpretation.

"History of Lucid Dreaming–Part 2." The Lucid Dreamer website.
Last accessed May 7, 2023. http://the-lucid-dreamer.com
/History-of-Lucid-Dreaming-2.html.

Kai-Ching Yu, Calvin. "Imperial Dreams and Oneiromancy in Ancient China—We Share Similar Dream Motifs with Our Ancestors Living Two Millenia Ago." *Dreaming: Journal of the International Association for the Study of Dreams* 32, no. 4 (March 2022): 364–74.

Khan, Molly. "Nott, the Dream Goddess of Night and Darkness." *Heathen at Heart* (blog). Last updated February, 25, 2019. https://www.patheos.com/blogs/heathenatheart/2019/02/nott-the-dream-goddess/.

Knight, Sirona, *Dream Magic: Night Spells and Rituals for Love, Prosperity, and Personal Power.* New York: Harper Collins, 2000.

Kracke, Waud H. "Cultural Aspects of Dreaming", *International Institute for Dream Research,* https://www.dreamresearch.ca/pdf/cultural.pdf.

LaBerge, Stephen. *Lucid Dreaming: A Concise Guide to Awakening in Your Dreams and in Your Life.* Boulder, CO: Sounds True Publishing, 2009.

Leaver, Samantha. "Hermes." In *Naming the God,* edited by Trevor Greenfield, 149–152. Winchester, UK: Moon Books, 2022.

Levrier, Katia, Andre Marchand, Genevieve Belleville, Beaulieu-Prevost Dominic, and Stephane Gray. "Nightmare Frequency, Nightmare Distress, and the Efficiency of Trauma Focused Cognitive Behavioral Therapy for Post-Traumatic Stress Disorder." *Archives of Trauma Research* 5, no. 3 (May 12, 2016). DOI: 10.5812/atr.33051.

Lloyd, Vanda. "Gwyn Ap Nudd." In *Naming the God,* edited by Trevor Greenfield, 139–142. Winchester, UK: Moon Books, 2022.

Mark, Emily. "Most Popular Gods & Goddesses of Ancient China." World History website. Updated

April 25, 2016. https://www.worldhistory.org/article/894
/most-popular-gods--goddesses-of-ancient-china/.

Marks, Hedy. "Dreams." WebMD website. November 5, 2021,
https://www.webmd.com/sleep-disorders/dreaming-overview.

Matthews, Caitlin. *Celtic Vision: Seership, Omens, and Dreams of the
Otherworld.* London: Watkins Publishing, 2012.

Matthews, Caitlin, and John Matthews. *The Encyclopedia of Celtic
Wisdom.* Rockport, MA: Element Books, 1994.

McKelvie, Callum, and Benjamin Radford. "Astral Projection: Facts
and Theories." Live Science website. February 25, 2022. https://
www.livescience.com/27978-astral-projection.html.

Moutinho, Sofia. "Are advertisers coming for your dreams?" *Science*
website. June 11, 2021. https://www.science.org/content
/article/are-advertisers-coming-your-dreams.

O'Brien, Lora. "Irish Pagan Magic–The 'Tarbh Feis.'" Lora O'Brien:
Irish Author and Guide website. July 24, 2018. https://
loraobrien.ie/irish-pagan-magic-tarbh-feis/.

Oxford Reference. "Imbas Forosnai." Last accessed August 2023.
https://www.oxfordreference.com/display/
10.1093/acref/9780198609674.001.0001
/acref-9780198609674-e-2760.

Paine, Angela. "Asclepius, God of Healing." In *Naming the God*,
edited by Trevor Greenfield, 102–105. Winchester, UK: Moon
Books, 2022.

Parkes, Veronica. "A Cycle of Life and Death-Slavic Goddesses
Morana and Vesna." Ancient Origins website. June 29, 2021.
https://www.ancient-origins.net/myths-legends
/morana-vesna-006984.

Payne, Kenn, "Hypnos." In *Naming the God*, edited by Trevor
Greenfield, 154–156. Winchester, UK: Moon Books, 2022.

"Pineal Gland." Cleveland Clinic website. Last reviewed June 22, 2022. https://my.clevelandclinic.org/health/body/23334-pineal-gland.

Prerna and Facty staff. "Identifying Sleep Apnea: 15 Key Symptoms and Risk Factors." Facty Health website. Last updated November 2, 2023. https://facty.com/ailments/sleep/10-symptoms-of-sleep-apnea/15/.

Raduga, Michael. "Predicting the Efficiency of Lucid Dreaming Practice." *Dreaming: Journal of the International Association for the Study of Dreams* 32, no. 4. (December 2022): 382–392.

Raman, Ryan. "African Dream Root: Compounds, Effects, Downsides, and More." Healthline website. April 15, 2021. https://www.healthline.com/nutrition/african-dream-root.

Rankine, David. "Anubis: The Jackal God." In *Naming the God*, edited by Trevor Greenfield, 95–97. Winchester, UK: Moon Books, 2022.

Ravenna, Morpheus. *The Book of the Great Queen: The Many Faces of the Morrigan from Ancient Legends to Modern Devotions*. Richmond, CA: Concrescent Press, 2015.

Regan, Sarah. "Everything You Need to Know About the 9th House and What It Means In Your Birth Chart." MBG Mindfulness website. December 20, 2022. https://www.mindbodygreen.com/articles/ninth-house-in-astrology.

Regula, DeTraci. *The Mysteries Of Isis: Her Worship and Magick*. St. Paul, MN: Llewellyn Publishing, 1999.

Rilke, Rainer Maria. *Letters to a Young Poet*, translated by Soren Filipski, Leipzig, Germany: Hythloday Press, 2014.

Rock, Andrea. *The Mind at Night: The New Science of How and Why We Dream*. New York: Basic Books, 2005.

Rodriguez, Emily. "Oneiromancy." *Britannica* website. Last updated April 22, 2016. https://www.britannica.com/topic/oneiromancy.

Roesler, Christian. "Jungian theory of dreaming and contemporary dream research–findings from the research project 'Structural Dream Analysis.'" *Analytical Psychology* 65, no. 1. (February 2020): 44–62. DOI: 10.1111/1468-5922.12566.

Roland, Elisa. "13 World Changing Ideas That Came From Dreams (Literally)." *Reader's Digest* website. Updated October 11, 2021. https://www.rd.com/list/ideas-that-came-from-dreams/.

Roric, Valda. "Ancient Gods—When Darkness Ruled the World." Ancient Origins website. Updated June 11, 2016. https://www.ancient-origins.net/myths-legends/ancient-gods-when-darkness-ruled-world-006067.

Saber, Indlieb Farazi. "While you were sleeping: The importance of dreams in Middle Eastern culture." Middle East Eye website. November 16, 2021. https://www.middleeasteye.net/discover/dreams-middle-east-civilisation-how-helped-define.

"Salvador Dali: The Persistence of Memory. 1931." Museum of Modern Art website. https://www.moma.org/audio/playlist/296/67.

Schredl, Michael, Carla Fuchs, and Remington Mallett. "Differences Between Lucid and Non-Lucid Dream Reports: A Within Subjects Design." *Dreaming: Journal of the International Association for the Study of Dreams* 32, no. 4 (2022): 345–52.

Shaw, Judith. "Caer Ibormeith: Celtic Goddess of Dreams and Prophecy." Feminism and Religion website. January 28, 2015. https://feminismandreligion.com/2015/01/28/caer-ibormeith-celtic-goddess-of-dreams-and-prophecy-by-judith-shaw/.

Shaw, Judith. "Elen of the Ways." Feminism and Religion website. September 28, 2016. https://feminismandreligion .com/2016/09/28/elen-of-the-ways-by-judith-shaw/.

Shetley, Susanna. "Increase Your Vibration With Essential Oils." *Smoky Mountain News* website. May 4, 2022. https://smokymountainnews.com/lifestyle/rumble /item/33553-increase-your-vibration-with-essential-oils.

"Sleep Terrors (Night Terrors)." Mayo Clinic website. Last updated January 13, 2024. https://www.mayoclinic.org /diseases-conditions/sleep-terrors/symptoms-causes/syc -20353524.

Smith, Andra M., and Claude Messier. "Voluntary Out-of-Body Experience: An fMRI Study." *Frontiers in Human Neuroscience* 8, no. 70 (2014): https://www.frontiersin.org/articles/10.3389 /fnhum.2014.00070/full.

Stefon, Matt. "Change." *Britannica* website. Last updated December 1, 2023. https://www.britannica.com/topic /Change-Chinese-deity.

Suni, Eric, and Alex Dimitriu. "Sleep Paralysis: Symptoms, Causes, and Treatment." Sleep Foundation website. August 14, 2023. https://www.sleepfoundation.org/parasomnias/sleep-paralysis.

Szpakowska, Kasia. "Dreams of Early Ancient Egypt." *American Society of Overseas Research* 10, no. 2 (February 2022): https:// www.asor.org/anetoday/2022/02/dreams-early-ancient-egypt/.

Taitel, Debra. "How to Effortlessly Dream Walk." Medium website. March 18, 2022. https://debratrtaitel.medium.com /how-to-effortlessly-dream-walk-cfbafe1cae34.

"The CIA's Gateway Report on Astral Projection and Templeton's Consciousness Competition." Mind Science website. April 13, 2021. https://mindscience.org/neuro-news/the-cias

-gateway-report-on-astral-projection-templetons
-consciousness-competition/.

Thelemapedia website. "Magick." Last updated Jan 21, 2022. http://
www.thelemapedia.org/index.php/Magick.

Tick, Edward. *The Practice of Dream Healing: Bringing Ancient
Greek Mysteries into Modern Medicine.* Wheaton, IL: Quest
Books, 2001.

Tuccillo, Dylan, Jared Zeizel, and Thomas Peisel. *A Field Guide to
Lucid Dreaming.* New York: Workman Publishing, 2013.

"'Twilight Author: It started with a dream." CNN website. November 18, 2009. https://edition.cnn.com/2009/LIVING
/worklife/11/18/o.twilight.newmoon.meyer/.

Van de Castle, Robert L., *Our Dreaming Mind,* New York: Ballantine Books, 1994.

Van Der Kolk, Bessel. *The Body Keeps the Score: Brain, Mind, and
Body in the Healing of Trauma.* New York: Penguin Books, 2014.

Walsh, Carl. "9 Inventions Inspired by Dreams." Bed Guru website.
November 2, 2016. https://www.bedguru
.co.uk/9-inventions-inspired-by-dreams.

Waggoner, Robert. "Exploring the Scientific Discovery of Lucid
Dreaming." *IONS 50* (blog), February 3, 2021. https://noetic
.org/blog/exploring-scientific-discovery-lucid-dreaming/.

Williams, Bethany. "Morpheus: The Greek God of Dreams and
Nightmares." The Collector website. March 29, 2022. https://
www.thecollector.com/morpheus-greek-god/.

Wu, Mingren. "Oneiromancy: Dream Predictions in Ancient Mesopotomia." Ancient Origins website. March 17, 2020. https://
www.ancient-origins.net/history-ancient-traditions
/oneiromancy-and-dream-predictions-ancient
-mesopotamia-005726.

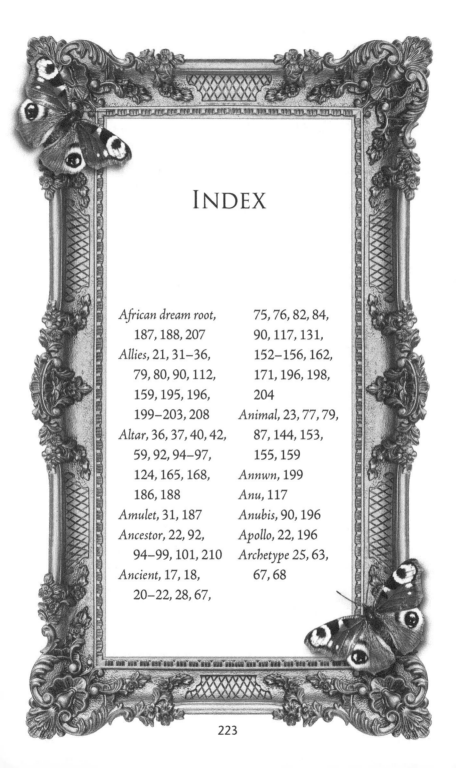

INDEX

To Write to the Author

If you wish to contact the author or would like more information about this book, please write to the author in care of Llewellyn Worldwide Ltd. and we will forward your request. Both the author and publisher appreciate hearing from you and learning of your enjoyment of this book and how it has helped you. Llewellyn Worldwide Ltd. cannot guarantee that every letter written to the author can be answered, but all will be forwarded. Please write to:

Robin Corak
℅ Llewellyn Worldwide
2143 Wooddale Drive
Woodbury, MN 55125-2989
Please enclose a self-addressed stamped envelope for reply,
or $1.00 to cover costs. If outside the U.S.A., enclose
an international postal reply coupon.

Many of Llewellyn's authors have websites with additional information and resources. For more information, please visit our website at http://www.llewellyn.com.